Pediatric Bipolar Spectrum Disorders

Pediatric Bipolar Spectrum Disorders

Elizabeth Burney Hamilton,
Kristie Knows His Gun, and Christina Tuning

MP **MOMENTUM** PRESS
HEALTH

MOMENTUM PRESS, LLC, NEW YORK

First published in 2017 by
Momentum Press, LLC
222 East 46th Street, New York, NY 10017
www.momentumpress.net

ISBN-13: 978-1-94474-933-0 (paperback)
ISBN-13: 978-1-94474-934-7 (e-book)

Momentum Press Child Clinical Psychology "Nuts and Bolts"
Collection

Cover and interior design by Exeter Premedia Services Private Ltd.,
Chennai, India

First edition: 2017

10 9 8 7 6 5 4 3 2 1

Printed in the United States of America.

Abstract

This volume is specifically designed to meet the needs of clinical practitioners seeking to better understand the complex needs of children and adolescents with bipolar spectrum disorders. Content is targeted toward psychologists, allied professionals, and advanced graduate students. This book is intended to provide clinicians with a comprehensive evidence-based assessment and treatment framework to optimally address the unique challenges faced by youth with mood disorders. Included are chapters on differential diagnoses, comorbid clinical issues, "state-of-the-art" evaluation techniques, and multimodal intervention strategies based in current research. Illustrative case histories are provided to further supplement practitioners' grasp of multifaceted issues involved in the assessment and treatment of this specialized population. Multiple resources and links to both evaluation and intervention protocols are provided for professionals to utilize within their clinical practice.

Keywords

adolescents, bipolar disorder, children, comorbidity, developmental psychopathology, evidence-based treatment, mood dysregulation, psychological assessment

Contents

Objectives of This Book

It is our goal to provide the practitioner working with pediatric bipolar spectrum disorders a summary of the most recent research findings to date, integrated with practical implications for clinical practice. This book is designed for clinical psychologists, allied mental health practitioners, and advanced graduate students who specialize in work with children and adolescents with pediatric onset bipolar spectrum disorder (PBSD). We have integrated current research with up-to-date practice guidelines to provide a framework for comprehensive assessment and treatment of this specialized population. Finally, we provide multiple case vignettes, which are based on de-identified composites of our clinical work, illustrating complex issues inherent in the diagnosis and treatment of PBSD.

CHAPTER 1

Description and Diagnosis

Ongoing advances in our understanding of bipolar spectrum disorders in children and adolescents are very encouraging to those of us working in the trenches. Throughout this volume we will refer to these disorders as Pediatric Bipolar Spectrum Disorders (PBSD), to reflect research indicating that: (1) bipolar disorder (BD) occurs across a spectrum, including the most severe forms as well as less extreme presentations, which nevertheless may be quite debilitating and often progress into Bipolar I (BD-I) or Bipolar II (BD-II) (Birmaher et al. 2014), and (2) pediatric symptom presentations often differ from adult manifestations, due to developmental processes (Demeter et al. 2013).

Recent efforts have sought to provide clinical criteria that can be optimally applied to the symptom presentations commonly seen in children and adolescents. First, although there is ongoing discussion about the actual number of youth presenting within the bipolar spectrum, there is now general international consensus that pediatric BD does occur (Carlson and Klein 2014; Goodwin et al. 2016). In fact, recent meta-analyses suggest there is a 1.8 to 2 percent prevalence of childhood-onset BD and there have been increases in the diagnosis of PBSD in both outpatient and inpatient settings, which may reflect the inclusion of broader spectrum disorders (Merikangas et al. 2012; Van Meter, Moreira, and Youngstrom 2011). Retrospective studies of adults with BD report that 10 to 20 percent had an onset before the age of 10 years and 60 percent had an onset before the age of 20 years (Diler and Birmaher 2012). Although there is some concern that rising rates of PBSD may reflect overly expansive inclusion of affective disturbances (Goodwin et al. 2016), increased rates of diagnoses may also indicate practitioners' growing awareness of developmentally determined symptoms, as well as advances in early identification (Frazier et al. 2014). There are attempts to delineate core bipolar symptoms in contrast to frequently occurring symptoms and comorbid presentations (Youngstrom and Algorta 2014).

Accumulating research has focused on developmentally specific symptom presentations in children and adolescents within the bipolar spectrum (Benarous et al. 2016a). The severe impact of PBSD is highlighted by its ranking as the fourth leading cause of disability among youth aged 10 to 24 years worldwide (Merikangas et al. 2011). PBSD is associated with numerous adverse outcomes that can hinder a youth's adaptive functioning, including problematic interpersonal relationships, impaired cognitive and academic performance, reoccurring utilization of health services, and a high rate of suicide attempts (Rizvi, Ong, and Youngstrom 2014). Early onset is specifically associated with more negative prognosis and poorer outcomes when compared to adult onset (Birmaher et al. 2014; Holtzman et al. 2015; Van Meter et al. 2016b). This difference may be due, in part, to the impairment this disorder creates within a child's maturational process, thus interfering with the acquisition of core skills and contributing to ongoing difficulties across adaptive domains (Van Meter et al. 2016b). Therefore, it is imperative that practitioners gain a holistic understanding of this disorder to enhance clinical practice and best meet the needs of the youth we serve.

Research, Diagnostic, and Treatment Systems

Challenges persist regarding optimal ways of describing, diagnosing, and treating pediatric mood disorders, while maintaining a lifespan perspective of illness course. We begin with a description of the major diagnostic systems utilized in the identification of PBSD. Then we review the different subtypes of BD and their diagnostic features, with particular emphasis on developmental factors. The importance of a developmental framework is shown by data indicating that although the average age of BD diagnosis is adolescence or early adulthood, prodromal symptoms are often present earlier (American Psychiatric Association [APA] 2013). Almost 80 percent of youth with PBSD will experience multiple recurrences (Birmaher et al. 2014), making it essential that the practitioner have awareness of age-based syndrome presentations to optimize ongoing interventions.

While there are other diagnostic models, we will focus on three frameworks that the professional working with PBSD is most likely to encounter:

1. International Classification of Diseases and Related Health Problems (ICD)
2. Diagnostic and Statistical Manual of Mental Disorders (DSM)
3. Research Domain Criteria (RDoC)

International Classification of Diseases and Related Health Problems

The International Classification of Diseases and Related Health Problems is a medical classification list established by the World Health Organization (WHO). Utilized by interdisciplinary professionals, it has been translated into 43 languages and is an internationally agreed diagnostic system of all diseases and other health problems (World Health Organization [WHO] 2016). As the need for more empirically sound and consistent diagnostic criteria has become evident, strides have been made to create congruence between the diagnostic frameworks of the ICD and DSM. Table 1.1 delineates the characteristic similarities and differences, as well as the convergences and divergences, of mood disorders between the Diagnostic and Statistical Manual-5th Edition (DSM-5) and proposed ICD-11. Ongoing updates can be found within the developing ICD, which has a projected release date of 2018 (WHO 2016). It is referred to as the Beta Draft and can be accessed at http://apps.who.int/classifications/icd11/browse/l-m/en

Diagnostic and Statistical Manual of Mental Disorders-5th Edition

The DSM-5 (APA 2013) has incorporated multiple changes intended to capture developmental variance in symptom presentation. Although the mood presentation of children and adolescents will often meet criteria for BD-I or BD-II within the DSM-5 framework, many youth within the bipolar spectrum will present with symptom constellations best described by the diagnostic categories of "other specified bipolar and related disorders" or "unspecified bipolar and related disorders". These diagnostic categories may capture complex mood disturbances which may not meet classification for BD-I or BD-II, due to developmental variations in symptom presentations.

Research Domain Criteria

The RDoC is a framework which integrates neurobiological, cognitive, and behavioral dimensions, across a continuum of adaptive functioning.

Table 1.1 Comparisons between DSM-5 and ICD-11 for mood disorders

Characteristics of mood disorders	DSM-5	ICD-11 (Beta version)
Taxonomy	Two separate categories for depressive disorders and bipolar disorders	One category (mood disorders) subdivided into depressive and bipolar
Dimensional measurements	Included to complement diagnosis and facilitate follow-up (i.e., depression, anger, or anxiety)	Not considered
Mixed anxiety-depressive disorders	Not included in the final version (very poor reliability in field studies); however, "anxiety" can be used as a specifier	Maintained
Grief	Removed as a criterion of exclusion for major depression	Maintained as a criterion of exclusion for diagnosis of major depression
"Mixed" depression	Depression can be diagnosed with specifier of mixed in unipolar depression	Not included
Temper tantrums	New diagnostic category: disruptive mood dysregulation disorder (DMDD)	Not included (a similar category was initially considered)
Convergences	**DSM-5**	**ICD-11 (Beta version)**
Increased activity or energy as a diagnostic criterion for hypo/mania	Included (as a requisite, unlike the DSM-IV)	Included (as a requisite, unlike the ICD-10)
Bipolar II	Maintained	Included as a specific category
Bipolar I, single manic episode	Maintained	Adopted (unlike the ICD-10)
Mania induced by treatments	Included (unlike the DSM-IV)	Maintained
Divergences	**DSM-5**	**ICD-11 (Beta version)**
Mixed episode	Used only as a specifier	Maintained
Bipolar spectrum	Criteria are operationalized (e.g., "other bipolar disorders")	Not considered
Other specifiers	Not included	Adds "childhood onset" specifier

Adapted from de Dios et al. (2014).

This dimensional approach expands on categorical systems of psychiatric diagnoses, while integrating developmental changes that impact illness course (see Garvey, Avenevoli, and Anderson 2016). The RDoC is transdiagnostic and reflects current research strategies for incorporating symptom clusters, and as such, is very applicable to describing pediatric bipolar spectrum disorders. The following five systems are included: (1) negative valence, (2) positive valence, (3) cognitive, (4) social processes, and (5) arousal or regulatory. The RDoC has been implemented by the National Institute of Mental Health (NIMH), which funds multiple pivotal studies on bipolar spectrum disorder in children and adolescents. For more detailed information, refer to: www.nimh.nih.gov/research-priorities/rdoc/index.shtml.

Summary of Research, Diagnostic, and Treatment Systems

In sum, guidelines across diagnostic frameworks recommend maintaining continuity of definitive core symptoms across the lifespan (Rizvi, Ong, and Youngstrom 2014). Although there should be congruence in definitions of mood states and clinical symptomatology across pediatric and adult populations, a developmental paradigm may allow the practitioner to interpret symptoms according to aged-based differences in clinical presentation. This focus is incorporated into developmental specifications within the DSM-5.

Classification of Bipolar Disorder Subtypes

The general population often holds misconceptions about the symptom presentation of BD. This may have been guided by portrayals in the media or memes used for entertainment value. Within popular culture, the term "bipolar" is often used as a descriptor for fleeting and intense behavioral switches between happy and sad moods. In actuality, the presence of depressive symptoms is needed for the diagnosis of BD-II and while this presentation is not necessary for BD-I, it is a common feature of the disorder. Depressive symptoms can reach the intensity level of a major depressive episode, or can manifest as "subthreshold" depression;

additionally, atypical depressive features are often apparent (Youngstrom and Algorta 2014).

It is also important to distinguish a manic episode from a hypomanic episode to accurately differentiate BD-I from other subtypes. A core distinction between these diagnostic subtypes is the *intensity*, not the *quality*, of symptoms (Youngstrom and Algorta 2014). A manic episode is severe and causes significant impairment in social or occupational functioning. The severity may require hospitalization in order to prevent harm to self or others, and psychotic features are often present (APA 2013).

With hypomania, the prefix "*hypo*" means "below" and refers to a less severe or less prolonged period of manic symptoms. Although hypomanic presentations may be more difficult to identify as they can appear as intense variations of normative functioning, they can, nevertheless, be debilitating over time. Hypomania differs from mania in three important ways (APA 2013):

1. Hypomania lasts at least four days but less than one week.
2. Although hypomania is associated with significant changes in adaptive functioning, there is less marked impairment than seen in full-blown mania.
3. Hypomania, of itself, rarely requires hospitalization; however, other symptoms of BD-II, which typically stem from the depressive episodes, may require hospitalization. These could include suicidality, repetitive self-injurious behavior, threats to others, or reckless behavior.

Throughout this volume, we utilize *hypo/mania* to encompass the spectrum of manic symptoms, while specifically distinguishing between full-blown manic episodes and hypomania when research indicates clinically important differences.

Figure 1.1 provides a visual representation of the symptom presentation for both BD-I and BD-II (note that a depressive episode is not required to meet the criteria for BD-I). Figure 1.2 gives a visual illustration of cyclothymia in contrast to both BD-I and BD-II. A detailed breakdown of the expressed mood episodes for the differing bipolar subtypes is shown in Table 1.2.

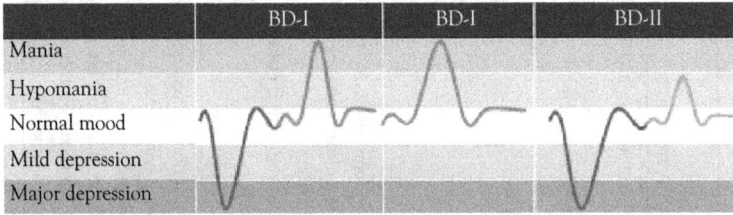

Figure 1.1 Mood episodes in BD-I and BD-II

Reprinted from Diler and Birmaher (2012).

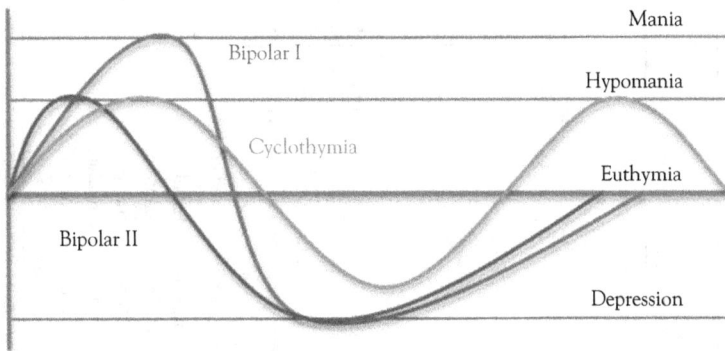

Figure 1.2 Bipolar disorder subtypes

Reprinted from http://neurowiki2013.wikidot.com/group:bipolar-neuroscience

Cyclothymia is a chronic and impairing subtype of BD, which typically has an insidious onset and persistent course (APA 2013). It is rarely
delineated in pediatric research, where it is commonly grouped with subthreshold presentations under the undifferentiated label "other specified
or unspecified BD" (Van Meter and Youngstrom 2012). Compared to
typically developing counterparts (TDC), youth with cyclothymia have
higher irritability, more comorbidity, greater sleep disturbances, and
higher rates of family history of BD (Van Meter et al. 2013). Further,
cyclothymic disorder is associated with a younger age of onset than BD-II
(Van Meter et al. 2013); within the mood-disordered pediatric population, the average age of cyclothymic symptom onset is 6.5 years (American
Psychiatric Association [APA], 2013). In a recent study, Van Meter et al.
(2016c) found that the irritability and impulsive aggressive behavior of
youth with cyclothymia was linked to impaired social functioning, at a
similar level of severity as youth with other BD subtypes.

Table 1.2 Description of bipolar subtypes

Bipolar subtypes	Manic symptoms	Hypomanic symptoms	Depressive symptoms
Bipolar I	• At least one manic episode • Lasts one week with symptoms present most of the day, nearly every day • Time duration waived if hospitalization is required due to severity of the mania • Noticeable change from baseline behavior • Distinct period of atypical and persistently elevated, expansive, or irritable mood along with persistently increased activity and energy	• May be present, but subsumed under full mania • Typically presents in BD-II, but manic symptoms are the cardinal distinction for this disorder	• Common in BD-I, but not required to meet criteria • Many individuals will experience a major depressive episodes during the course of their lives

Bipolar II	• Not present	• At least one hypomanic episode, lasting at least four consecutive days with symptoms present most of the day, nearly every day
		• Noticeable change from baseline behavior
		• Distinct period of elevated, expansive, or irritable mood and increased energy
			• At least one major depressive episode
			• Symptoms include a distinct change from previous functioning
			• At least one of the symptoms is either
			  1. depressed mood or
			  2. loss of interest or pleasure

Cyclothymia	• Not present	• For children, at least one full year with periods of hypomanic symptoms • Hypomanic symptoms present for at least half the time and the individual has not been without the symptoms for more than two months at a time	• For children, at least one full year with periods of depressive symptoms • Depressive periods present for at least half the time and the individual has not been without the symptoms for more than two months at a time

Adapted from the DSM-5, American Psychiatric Association (2013).

Ongoing research indicates that many children and adolescents present with substantial mood disturbances that do not fully meet diagnostic criteria for BD-I, BD-II, or cyclothymia, but symptoms create clinically significant distress or impairment or both (Hafeman et al. 2013; Fristad and Algorta 2013). DSM-5 provides the categories of "Other Specified Bipolar and Related Disorders" (when the clinician chooses to communicate specific reasons criteria are not met) and "Unspecified Bipolar and Related Disorders" (when the clinician chooses not to specify why criteria are not met) (APA 2013). The ICD also includes a "BD, Unspecified" category. Developmental differences in mood disorder presentation may contribute to the relatively high rates of children and adolescents initially meeting criteria for "other or unspecified" bipolar diagnoses. Support for conceptualizing mood disorders through a spectrum framework is provided by ongoing evidence indicating continuity across bipolar diagnostic categories. Youth with other specified or unspecified bipolar disorders are similar to those with more severe BD diagnoses in family history, age of onset, illness duration, symptom severity, functional impairment, and rates of comorbidity (Hafeman et al. 2013). Further, longitudinal studies indicate that approximately half of youth with other specified or unspecified BD or cyclothymia convert to BD-I or II across a five-year follow-up, particularly when there is a positive family illness history (Axelson et al. 2011; Birmaher et al. 2009).

As stated earlier, throughout this book we have chosen to use PBSD to describe the full range of child and adolescent presentations, encompassing BD-I, BD-II, cyclothymia, and "other or unspecified" BDs. Variability in findings across different studies is likely due in large part to methodological differences in diagnostic criteria for pediatric BD (Fristad and Algorta 2013). It has been our goal to synthesize research to date, while also specifying, when possible, specific diagnostic classifications utilized in each study.

Behavioral Presentations

Pediatric BD is characterized by mood fluctuations and changes in energy levels that are clearly outside the child's normative baseline (Van Meter et al. 2016a). Up to 70 percent of youth with PBSD show elated, expansive, or euphoric moods that are developmentally uncharacteristic (see Tables 1.3 and 1.4). During the diagnostic process it is important to evaluate symptom presentation through the lens of a child's environmental and cultural context, while also ruling out possible effects of medications or substance use. Although mood symptoms typically hinder the youth's daily functioning, it should be noted that moderate levels of hypomania may actually enhance a child's cognitive and interpersonal skills (Birmaher 2013).

A particular diagnostic challenge for children and adolescents within the bipolar spectrum is that their mood fluctuations tend to be more fluid and diffuse, and less differentiated than those of adults. While the existence of hypo/mania must be present for the diagnosis of PBSD, the presentation within children and adolescents can both overlap and differentiate from that of adults. By definition, a manic episode refers to, "a discrete period of elevated, expansive, or irritable mood and increased level of energy and activity" (APA 2013, p. 127). A meta-analysis of children and adolescents revealed that the three most highly reported symptoms of a manic episode include increased energy, irritable mood, and grandiosity, similar to symptom patterns found in adults (Rizvi et al. 2014). Table 1.4 presents a summary of core clinical symptoms described in terms of their relative *sensitivity* in identifying PBSD and relative *specificity* in distinguishing PBSD from other psychiatric disorders in children and adolescents.

Beyond the elevated energy characteristic of PBSD, additional behavioral presentations are unique to this developmental population. For instance, during manic episodes, children and adolescents typically display an irritable mood, often described as touchy, angry, oppositional, or reactive. Further, in comparison to adolescents, younger children with BD evidence more irritability (Birmaher et al. 2009), and this can take the presentation of being grouchy or easily set off, throwing tantrums, crying, throwing objects, and acting physically aggressive toward others. It is important to note that transient irritability is a typical and developmentally appropriate mood state for children and adolescents. However, a distinct feature of youth with bipolar spectrum disorder is that their irritability will often manifest as anger or self-injurious behavior, extreme rages, or meltdowns (Topor et al. 2013). Approximately 81 percent of youth with this disorder show a noticeable increase of this behavioral presentation (see Tables 1.3 and 1.4).

By definition, the criteria of mania is met if three (or more) of the following symptoms (four if the mood is only irritable) are present to a significant degree and represent a noticeable change from usual behavior (APA 2013). Tables 1.3 and 1.4 provide a detailed description of the following symptomology and the differential presentations they can elicit. These symptoms can be remembered by using the acronym GRAPES+D (Diler and Birmaher 2012).

- **G**randiosity or inflated self-esteem
- **R**acing thoughts or flight of ideas
- **A**ctivity level increase or psychomotor agitation
- **P**ressured speech or excessive talkativeness
- **E**xcessive involvement in potentially harmful activities
- **S**leep Disturbance
- **D**istractibility

As shown in Table 1.3 and 1.4, for children and adolescents, grandiosity, decreased sleep, and high-risk sexual activity are relatively specific indicators of PBSD, particularly within the hypo/manic phases (Youngstrom, Birmaher, and Findling 2008). Clearly, the presence of these symptoms should be interpreted within a developmental context, in comparison to age-appropriate frequency and intensity.

Cognitive Features

Youth with bipolar spectrum disorders often display significant neurocognitive deficits when compared to TDCs (Van Meter et al. 2016b). Some of the most notable impairments fall within verbal learning and memory, which emerge within tasks requiring language comprehension and auditory processing (Schenkel et al. 2012). Additionally, deficits have been found in executive functioning (EF), which includes the ability to plan, organize, and inhibit behavior. Further, youth with PBSD experience dysfunction in selective attention, sustained attention, behavioral inhibition, processing speed, working memory, visuospatial memory, visual-motor

Table 1.3 *Behavioral presentation of mania*

Behavioral presentation	Percentage of symptom	Description of behaviors	Examples	Differential presentations
Grandiosity or inflated self-esteem	Grandiosity: 57 percent Euphoric or elated mood: 64 percent	High self-esteem, self-confidence, and self-importance	• Jumping off house or "flying" from a tree • Older youth might tell their coach how to run the team or tell their teacher how to instruct the class • Overall, behaviors that most youth would not dare attempt	• Difficult to assess due to the normative developmental process of youth's overestimations of their abilities • Identifying a change from usual behavior and self-image is key for an accurate diagnosis
Racing thoughts or flight of ideas	Racing thoughts: 61 percent Flight of ideas: 54 percent	Internal thought processes occur too quickly to articulate	• Jumping from one topic to another, in a scattered manner that is difficult to follow	• The distinction between PBSD and attention-deficit/hyperactivity disorder (ADHD) focuses on whether the symptoms are episodic (PBSD) or chronic (ADHD)
Activity level increase or psychomotor agitation	Increased energy: 79 percent Goal-directed activity: 72 percent Hyperactive: 62 percent	Activities are typically impulsive with poor planning and execution	• Youth may begin ambitious projects, but struggle to complete them • Psychomotor agitation may appear as hyperactive, restless, or impulsive	• For PBSD, behaviors must be exaggerated, represent a distinct change from their baseline, and be recognized by others as excessive for developmental age
Pressured speech or excessive talkativeness	Pressured speech: 63 percent	Speech is typically fast, loud, and difficult to understand	• "Knight's move thinking," youth jumps between topics without connecting spaces	• Rate of speech is typically an attempt to keep up with the racing thoughts • Just as thoughts jump from topic to topic, so do rapid transitions of speech • In children, this is also expressed in a concrete manner

Symptom			
Excessive involvement in potentially harmful activities	Poor judgment: 61 percent; Inappropriate laughter: 57 percent	Pleasurable and reckless activities that may result in negative consequences; can also manifest as hypersexual behavior	• Children may perform reckless stunts, for example, with their bikes or skateboards • Older youth may engage in alcohol or drug consumption, stealing, spending too much money, or driving recklessly • May experience uncontrollable laughter after unfortunate events • Hypersexual behavior must be developmentally inappropriate, and not due to exposure of sexualized videos, TV, or actual sexual acts • Children with PBSD express hypersexual behavior with an erotic, pleasure-seeking quality • Children who have been abused express this behavior in an anxious, compulsive nature
Sleep disturbance	Decreased need for sleep: 56 percent	Need for sleep profoundly reduced from baseline, with no consequential fatigue	• May stay awake into the early morning hours performing activities such as, rearranging furniture, watching TV, playing video games, social media, or wandering the house • Youth with PBSD will likely engage in activities into the early morning hours • Youth with insomnia will likely lie in bed trying to obtain sleep
Distractibility	Distractibility: 74 percent	Difficulty initiating and maintaining focus and attention	• Unable to concentrate on schoolwork or complete chores • Disorganized • Flighty • Youth with PBSD experience a marked change from their baseline functioning • Youth with ADHD have more persistent and pervasive symptomatology
Mood lability or irritability	Mood lability: 76 percent; Irritability: 77 percent	Fluctuations of mood, or mood swings, that are exaggerated or an inappropriate emotional reaction to benign stimuli	• Angry or behavioral outbursts, such as throwing or destroying objects • Excessive crying that is inappropriate for the situation • May be difficult to distinguish PBSD from DMDD • Focusing on the prevalence of manic symptoms *other than irritability and tantrums* can help distinguish PBSD from DMDD
Hypomania		Symptoms are less severe in duration and intensity than in full mania	• Rather than causing a disruption of daily living, may actually increase functioning in some areas, including academia and interpersonal relationships • Hypomania can be distinguished from mania as it does not cause significant impairment or hospitalization • If the severity level requires hospitalization, mania is likely to be the accurate diagnosis

Adapted from Van Meter et al. (2016a). Additional information adapted from Birmaher (2013); APA (2013); Rizvi et al. (2014).

Table 1.4 Sensitivity and specificity of clinical symptoms of PBSD

Clinical symptom	PBSD sensitivity (%)	PBSD specificity level	Differential diagnostic considerations
Elated, expansive, euphoric mood	70	High	Substance or medication use
Irritable mood	81	Low	Oppositional defiant disorder (ODD), DMDD, unipolar depression
Grandiosity	78	Moderate	Conduct disorder (CD), substance use, psychotic disorder
Increased energy	89*	Moderate	ADHD
Distractibility	84	Low	ADHD, neurological conditions
Pressured speech	82	Unclear	ADHD
Racing thoughts	74	Good	Expressive language disorder, substance or medication use, psychotic disorders
Decreased need for sleep	72	High	Distinguish need versus sleep disturbance common to other diagnoses
Poor judgment	69	Moderate	ADHD, developmental delays
Flight of ideas	56	Moderate	Language disorder, substance or medication use
Hypersexuality	38	High	Sexual trauma
Mood swings or lability	High	High	Substance or medication use, neurological conditions, disruptive disorders

Adapted from Youngstrom, Birmaher, and Findling (2008).
Note: Sensitivity percentiles are given as averages of ranges.
*Highest sensitivity in meta-analysis.

skills, reversal learning, and information processing for emotionally valenced words (Dickstein et al. 2016; Lera-Miguel et al. 2015; Walshaw, Alloy, and Sabb 2010). Research has found that these delays in cognitive performance are an ongoing concern across the developmental trajectory (Lera-Miguel et al. 2015). Additional information regarding neurocognitive features is discussed in greater depth in Chapter 2.

Psychotic symptoms, while not reported in all cases of pediatric bipolar, are the most severe features occurring within this disorder (Lera-Miguel et al. 2015). Research has found rates of psychotic symptoms ranging from 14 to 73.3 percent, with many studies finding increased psychosis in BD-I (see Carlson and Pataki 2015). Results from the Treatment of Early Age Mania (TEAM) study found that within a sample of youth with BD-I, 73.3 percent experienced psychosis, including 38.9 percent with delusions (most commonly of grandiosity), 5.1 percent with pathological hallucinations, and 32.3 percent with both (Tillman et al. 2008). Additionally, rates of psychotic symptoms were comparable between those aged 6 to 9 years and those aged 10 to 16 years. In contrast to the more frequently noted auditory hallucinations in adults, visual hallucinations were the most prevalent pathological psychotic symptom in this child and adolescent sample.

With the exception of findings from the TEAM study (Tillman et al. 2008), most studies have found that, overall, adolescents with PBSD have higher rates of psychotic symptoms than do children (see Carlson and Pataki 2015; Topor et al. 2013). Typically, youth with PBSD experience psychosis during a mood episode, either depressive or manic. When the psychosis extends beyond the mood episodes, the presentation is indicative of schizophrenia, or a related disorder (see Carlson and Pataki 2015). It is possible that psychotic symptoms may index illness severity rather than distinct subtype of BD. For example, recent Australian findings indicated comparable rates of psychosis between youth with BD-I and II (Hirneth et al. 2015).

When youth first experience psychosis it can be difficult to distinguish the presentation as pediatric bipolar rather than early onset schizophrenia, major depression, or anxiety disorders, including posttraumatic stress disorder (PTSD). Assessing psychotic features can be particularly difficult in children and adolescents due to their normative developmental stages. For instance, children typically experience magical thinking or unusual beliefs and adolescents often endorse the "personal fable," their conviction that they are extraordinary and invulnerable to mistakes, accidents, and illnesses (Youngstrom and Algorta 2014).

Emotional Dysregulation

As previously stated, the core features of PBSD involve pathological dysregulation of mood and energy, which typically ranges from elation and irritability to severe depression (Youngstrom and Algorta 2014). Although, hypo/mania is the hallmark of bipolar disorder, youth with PBSD typically spend more time in a depressed state (Rizvi et al. 2014). In fact, the initial presentation is usually depression with combined hyperactivity, followed by mania (American Academy of Child and Adolescent Psychiatry 2007). A recent meta-analysis of initial prodromal periods revealed that depressive, rather than manic symptoms, were the core features of the initial mood episode reported by patients with BD (Van Meter et al. 2016b). Additionally, longitudinal results from the Course and Outcome of Bipolar Illness in Youth (COBY) study found that although the majority of youth fully recovered from their initial episode (81.5 percent), 2.5 years after this onset more than half (62.5 percent) had syndromal recurrence, particularly including depression and mixed symptoms (Birmaher et al. 2009).

For diagnosis, depressive symptoms must exceed developmentally typical expressions and must cluster into episodes (Birmaher 2013). These depressive episodes may also be marked by atypical presentations, including hypersomnia or insomnia, increased or decreased appetite, weight gain or loss, substantially decreased energy, and hypersensitivity to rejection (Youngstrom and Algorta 2014). It is also important to note that assessing depressive episodes may be difficult due to the child's cognitive and emotional immaturity. For instance, younger children may lack the ability to accurately report what they are feeling and instead may describe "boredom" or "irritability." Additionally, the external display of depression may be perceived as behavior problems, including oppositionality and defiance, leading to misinterpretation of these symptoms (Birmaher 2013).

Irritability is an extremely common symptom of this disorder among youth, in both hypo/manic and depressive phases, as seen in Tables 1.3 and 1.4. Younger children may express irritability through protracted temper tantrums, while older children and adolescents display emotional outbursts or "affective storms," that arise with little provocation. It is important to note that irritability does not have high specificity to pediatric bipolar, as it is seen in many disorders; however, its absence may decrease the likelihood of a bipolar diagnosis (Diler and Birmaher 2012).

Behavior symptom presentations also differ between children and adolescents. It has been found that mood lability is particularly characteristic of childhood onset bipolar. This lability refers to the rapid fluctuations of mood within a brief period of time, which appears to be internally driven regardless of environmental influences. These fluctuations, along with the expression of irritability and anger, distinguish children from adolescents, as adolescents with bipolar will tend to show more adult-like symptomatology, which includes more defined manic and depressive episodes (Diler and Birmaher 2012).

Risk for suicide among individuals with bipolar disorders is estimated to be at least 15 times higher than that found within the general population (APA 2013). The strongest risk factor for suicidality among children and adolescents is the diagnosis of a psychiatric disorder, specifically bipolar (Hauser, Galling, and Correll 2013), and suicidal ideation and attempts may occur across all BD subtypes and developmental stages (Hirneth et al. 2015). PBSD has one of the highest rates of suicide completion of all mental disorders (Ellis et al. 2014). Although suicide completion in youth is lower than in adults, ideation and attempt are relatively common in youth (Hauser, Galling, and Correll 2013). Research shows that approximately 20 to 30 percent of youth with PBSD report suicide attempts and over 50 percent report one or more periods of suicidal ideations (Ellis et al. 2014). In contrast to preadolescents, older youth have more suicide attempts, which may be due to having a greater access to a means or being less supervised than younger children (Hauser, Galling, and Correll 2013). However, even among children with PBSD, over 41 percent endorse suicidal ideation, with over 30 percent reporting active suicidality (Weinstein et al. 2015). Additionally, a real intent to commit suicide may be masked by the methods chosen by young children, as their methods typically lack lethality as they may hold their breath or put their head under water in the bathtub (Birmaher 2013).

Summary of Symptom Presentation Across Domains

While we separated the behavioral, cognitive, and emotional features of pediatric bipolar for clarity of content, it is important to note that symptoms are fluid and they frequently overlap across domains. Therefore, expert consensus recommends using FIND (*Frequency*, *Intensity*, *Number*, and *Duration*) as a guideline to identify the clinical significance of a behavior or a symptom (Kowatch et al. 2009). This acronym of criteria specificity will be discussed in greater depth in Chapter 4.

Diagnostic Features of Bipolar Disorders

Epidemiology

An international meta-analysis found an overall rate of PBSD of 1.8 percent, while prevalence estimated in youth 12 years and older may be as high as 2.7 percent (Van Meter, Moreira, and Youngstrom 2011). No differences were found in rates reported from different countries, although a wider *range* of rates was found in the U.S. studies, while different rates across studies were primarily due to variations in diagnostic criteria (Van Meter, Moreira, and Youngstrom 2011). Further, base rates of PBSD in different treatment settings range from 5 to 10 percent in outpatient and community mental health settings, to 15 to 20 percent in specialty outpatient centers, up to 25 to 40 percent in inpatient settings, as summarized by Youngstrom et al. (2012).

A careful review of ethnic and racial factors indicates that PBSD presents at comparable rates across diverse populations (APA 2013), although ethnic minorities are more likely to have higher rates of misdiagnosis than their Anglo peers (Liang, Matheson, and Douglas 2016). Cultural factors, which will be discussed further in Chapter 2, likely contributed to differential diagnostic rates reported in the past. However, when clinicians utilize structured diagnostic interviews, standardized assessment tools, and evidence-based models for interpreting risk factors and rating scales, PBSD rates across diverse groups are similar, as discussed in Chapter 3 (Pendergast et al. 2015).

Longitudinal results from the COBY study indicate that a more severe illness course is associated with earlier age of onset of mood symptoms, family history of mood disorder, higher rates of subsyndromal symptoms and comorbid disorders, increased exposure to negative life events, and lower socioeconomic status (Birmaher et al. 2009; Birmaher et al. 2014). COBY participants, ages 7 to 17 years, had longer symptomatic stages and more frequent cycling (changing from one mood to another) or mixed episodes (meeting the diagnostic criteria for both mania and major depression) when compared to adult patterns (Birmaher et al. 2009). In addition, these youth were more likely to transition to a more severe form of bipolar over the course of their illness, and at a higher rate, when compared to adults.

Although the peak age of onset of BD is during the adolescent period, emerging data suggests that elementary age children, and even younger, may present with classically defined bipolar symptoms (see Demeter et al. 2013). Prepubertal children with PBSD have more mixed episodes, less complete remissions, and more mood shifts, while adolescent onset symptomatology is similar to adults (DeFilippis and Wagner 2015). In contrast to prepubertal children, older youth are more likely to exhibit higher levels of depressed mood, while energy levels and aggression decrease slightly with age (Demeter et al. 2013).

Gender distribution of PBSD across international samples appears fairly equivalent, similar to adult patterns (APA 2013; Kessing, Vradi, and Andersen 2015), although there may be differences in symptom *expression* between males and females. For example, Youngstrom and Algorta (2014) found that younger males show higher rates of mania while adolescent females express higher rates of depression. There is some evidence of gender differences in the *prominence* of symptoms that initiate referral for PBSD, with externalizing symptoms more salient in males, and internalizing symptoms more salient in females (Merikangas et al. 2012).

In summary, ongoing epidemiological studies are providing evidence that PBSD has similar prevalence rates to adults, and is equally common across gender, ethnic and racial groups. More severe PBSD course is associated with earlier age of symptom onset and index mood episode (Birmaher et al. 2014). Finally, while international meta-analysis found that bipolar can have a childhood onset, the prevalence increases during adolescence (Van Meter, Moreira, and Youngstrom 2011).

Differential Diagnoses

Sophia is an 11-year-old girl who has been experiencing intermittent episodes of increased activity, "silliness," creativity, poor concentration, and inflated self-esteem, along with a lack of need for sleep, without noticeable tiredness the next day. She has also had periods lasting 3 to 5 weeks during which she becomes more withdrawn, irritable, sad, tired, tearful, and distractible, with less motivation and more defiant behaviors both at home and school. This symptom pattern has lasted for approximately the past two years. Sophia was diagnosed with ADHD last year by her family practitioner and has participated in individual and family psychotherapy, along with maintaining medication compliance of stimulants prescribed by her pediatrician. However, symptoms have exacerbated, rather than decreased.

As this vignette demonstrates, one factor that significantly increases the difficulty of accurate diagnosis is the commonality of PBSD's core features with those of other disorders. For instance, bipolar depressive episodes and unipolar depressive episodes have commonality between symptom presentations. Yet, in contrast to unipolar depression, bipolar depression often has higher levels of severity and impairment, along with patterns of psychiatric comorbidity and heritability which allow the clinician to differentiate between these disorders (Uchida et al. 2015). Accurate differential diagnosis of PBSD is crucial as diagnosis guides treatment, including psychotherapeutic and pharmacological interventions. Misdiagnosis has the potential to exacerbate symptoms, particularly within the realm of psychopharmacotherapy. Inaccurate or delayed diagnosis may result in an increase in the frequency and severity of mood episodes, while also hindering the benefits of appropriate treatment (Van Meter et al. 2016b).

Differential diagnosis can be improved by evaluating the relative *sensitivity* versus *specificity* of the symptom to PBSD, which is addressed in Table 1.4. Table 1.5 summarizes distinct and common features of PBSD to other psychiatric disorders with overlapping symptomatology. Finally, additional information distinguishing behaviors associated with PBSD from similar behaviors found in ADHD and CD is shown in Table 1.6.

Comorbidity and Correlates

Pediatric bipolar often occurs with comorbid psychiatric symptoms (Joshi and Wilens 2015). Table 1.7 describes some of these common co-occurring disorders. The phenotype of PBSD may be similar to other childhood disorders, causing an overlap in expressed symptomatology which complicates accurate differential diagnosis. Further, the early identification

Table 1.5 *Differential features of diagnoses with overlapping symptoms with PBSD*

Differential diagnosis	Distinct core features	Common core features
Attention-deficit/hyperactivity disorder	Following features are common in PBSD, but rare in ADHD: • **Early discriminators:** Elevated mood, decreased need for sleep • **Later discriminators:** Appetite changes, physical complaints, sadness, hypersexuality, and suicidal ideations • Irritability and decreased frustration tolerance common in both, but often more severe and frequent in PBSD • Impulsivity and hyperactivity are consistent across time in ADHD, but fluctuate with mood states in PBSD	• Hyperactivity, impulsivity, and decreased attention span are common across both disorders, but frequency and duration can help differentiate these disorders
Disruptive behavioral disorders	• ODD and CD patterns are repetitive and persistent • PBSD is episodic in nature	• Dysregulated behavior is a common feature of PBSD and disruptive behavioral disorders
Substance use	• Mood and behavioral dysregulation are present in an episodic manner in PBSD • For substance use, the usage can cause the same behavioral features, but these features are contingent to the use of the substance	• Erratic mood and behavior are common effects of multiple substances and common features of PBSD • Careful examination of time sequence will help distinguish whether medication or substance is creating mood or behavioral activation, or exposing a bipolar diathesis
Depressive disorders	• Depressive symptoms are a core feature of PBSD	• Since many youth within the bipolar spectrum initially present with depressive symptoms, careful review of family loadings and developmental factors is needed

(Continued)

Table 1.5 *Differential features of diagnoses with overlapping symptoms with PBSD*   (Continued)

Differential diagnosis	Distinct core features	Common core features
Disruptive mood dysregulation disorder	The following are found in PBSD, but not in DMDD: • Hypo/mania • Psychotic symptoms • Differential response to medication • DMDD has a differential trajectory, often transitioning to unipolar depression or anxiety disorders	• Irritability and lack of emotional regulation are common in youth with PBSD and DMDD
Trauma and abuse	• Although both PBSD and trauma disorders are marked by negative mood and by high levels of arousal and reactivity, trauma disorders have an identifiable stressor which is clearly linked to changes in cognitions and emotional reactivity	• Emotional dysregulation is a common symptom of youth with significant trauma histories and PBSD; there is also an intricate relationship between PBSD and trauma • First, families with bipolar disorder may be chaotic and unpredictable, leading to a series of traumatic events for the child with PBSD • Second, the challenges of coping effectively with a child with PBSD may create secondary trauma within the family system

Adapted from Post, Findling, and Luckenbaugh (2014); Rizvi, Ong, and Youngstrom (2014); Pavuluri and May (2014); Frias, Palma, and Farriols (2014a); Youngstrom and Algorta (2014); Arango, Fraguas, and Parellada (2014).

Table 1.6 *Characteristic behavioral presentation associated with PBSD, ADHD, and CD*

Behavioral presentation	PBSD	ADHD	CD
Self-esteem	Inflated	Inflated or deflated or both	Inflated or deflated or both
Pleasure	Euphoric in mania Dysphoric in mixed or depressed state	Often dysphoric or euthymic	Pleasure in violating societal norms, especially if not caught
Attention	Distractible	Distractible	Normal to vigilant
Hyperactivity	Goal directed	Unproductive	Goal directed
Sleep	Episodic disturbances such as decreased need in mania	Chronic poor sleep; often late bedtimes	Not known to be disrupted except with substance abuse
Speech	Pressured or rapid in mania; slow in depression	Often rapid; may be pressured	Typically, within normal limits
Impulsivity	Externally driven; reactionary	Internally driven	May have predatory or reactionary acts
Social	Often good	Often poor	Often poor
Academic	Often good	Often poor	Often poor
Psychomotor activity	Agitated in mania or mixed states; retarded in depressed states	Chronically agitated	Easily agitated

Adapted Bernstein and Pataki (2015); emedicine.medscape.com/article/913464-treatment.

Table 1.7 Diagnoses commonly comorbid with PBSD

Comorbid diagnoses	Percentage of comorbidity with PBSD	Diagnostic implications of comorbidities
Attention-deficit/hyperactivity disorder	Ranges from 60 to 93 percent	• Manic and mood episodes of PBSD are more severe with greater frequency and duration • Comorbidity with ADHD is typically associated with early-onset bipolar • Prepubescent onset bipolar has the highest rate of comorbidity, while adolescent and adulthood onset have the lowest rate
Disruptive behavior disorders	Ranges from 7 to 75 percent Oppositional defiant disorder specifically: ranges from 47 to 88 percent	• Significant increase in the recurrence of both depressive and manic episodes • Reduction in their response to treatment • Hospitalized samples are associated with poorer symptom recovery • In CD specifically, it is not clearly known if stealing, lying, or vandalizing are due to the disinhibition of mania including impulsivity, irritability, and grandiosity, or are comorbid with PBSD
Substance use disorders	Ranges from 16 to 48 percent	• Adolescents with early onset bipolar have the highest risk for comorbidity • Experience an impaired neurocognitive profile with a decrease in global functioning, especially within legal and academic domains • Longer duration and recovery from depression and manic episodes
Pervasive developmental disorders	Ranges from 11 to 30 percent	• Overlapping symptoms of aggression and severe mood disturbances found within youth who have a high incidence of bipolar in their family • PBSD and autism spectrum disorder have similar phenotypic features including symptom profile, pattern of comorbidity, and measures of functioning

Anxiety disorders	Ranges from 41 to 80 percent	• Anxious symptoms are not included within the criteria of depression or mania. Therefore, the clinician needs to determine if the specifier of "with anxious distress" should be used, or if a comorbid diagnosis of anxiety is warranted • More severe depressive symptoms, longer or greater affective episodes, and more severe impairment in global functioning • Increased mood recurrences, prolonged time to reach recovery, less euthymic once recovery is reached, and a greater number of cycling and depressive episodes
Panic disorders	Occurs in approximately 23 percent	• Suggested that panic disorder with bipolar is due to a genetic subtype of the bipolar disorder • Tend to have a stronger bias toward threats when compared to nonanxious pediatric bipolar youth
Posttraumatic stress disorders	Occurs in approximately 16 percent	• Significant increase in the occurrence of PTSD among a group of older adolescents with bipolar disorder, when compared to TDC • Higher risk of substance use disorder was found in adolescents with PBSD and comorbid PTSD
Obsessive-compulsive disorders	Occurs in approximately 39 percent	• Experience an earlier age of onset for OCD and significantly more impairment • Bipolar symptomatology exacerbates OCD symptomology, causing an increase in the frequency of obsessions • Overlapping of symptoms between disorders, including agitation, racing thoughts, feelings of distress, increased goal directed behavior, and repetitive or unwanted hypersexual thoughts, can complicate the delineation of these disorders

Adapted from Walshaw, Alloy, and Sabb (2010); Frias, Palma, and Farriols (2014a); Youngstrom and Algorta (2014); Joshi and Wilens (2015); Yen et al. (2016); Van Meter, Moreira, Youngstrom (2011).

of comorbid disorders is crucial in order to implement comprehensive treatment and enhance therapeutic outcomes (Frias, Palma, and Farriols 2014a).

As seen in Table 1.7, the most common comorbid conditions with PBSD include ADHD, disruptive behavior disorders, substance use disorders, pervasive developmental disorders and anxiety disorders including panic disorder, PTSD, and obsessive compulsive disorder (OCD) (Biederman et al. 2013a; Joshi and Wilens 2015). Comorbid anxiety disorders can exacerbate BD symptomatology and create a poorer prognosis and trajectory (Frias, Palma, and Farriols 2014a). Additionally, behavioral disorders, including ADHD, ODD, and CD are particularly comorbid among preadolescent males with PBSD (Rajakannan et al. 2014). Furthermore, an international survey administered by the WHO revealed that patterns of comorbidity were similar internationally (see Joshi and Wilens 2015). Lastly, it is important to note that the emotional dysregulation and behavioral disruption present in many of the child and adolescent disorders may reflect a prodromal pathway to PBSD.

Summary Recommendations for Diagnosis

In sum, the competent practitioner will seek to provide an accurate and comprehensive diagnosis, while taking into account a broad range of symptomatology, as interpreted through a developmental framework. Although this may involve the use of codiagnostic categories, it is important to distinguish whether symptom patterns can best be explained under the primary umbrella category of PBSD, or whether ongoing clinical presentations warrant the inclusion of a comorbid diagnosis. A simple guideline is to evaluate what additional symptoms remain persistently even when the mood disorder is well-regulated.

Practitioner Summary of Description and Diagnosis of PBSD

1. PBSD is ranked as the fourth leading cause of disability among youth aged 10 to 24 years worldwide and is associated with numerous adverse outcomes.

2. BD-I, BD-II, cyclothymia, and "other or unspecified" are the specific subtypes of PBSD, with multiple commonalities, as well as distinct expressions of symptomatology.

3. Symptoms in PBSD are fluid and frequently overlap across domains, including behavioral, cognitive, and emotional factors.

4. PBSD has similar prevalence rates to adults, and is equally common across gender, ethnic and racial groups, although symptoms should be evaluated within a culturally-sensitive framework.

5. Accurate diagnosis of PBSD requires that the practitioner carefully consider both:

    a. The commonality of core diagnostic features with other psychiatric disorders.

    b. Frequent comorbid disorders, including depressive disorders, anxiety disorders, ADHD, and disruptive behavior disorders.

6. A developmental framework should be utilized in order to evaluate whether symptoms are normative variations of child and adolescent behavior, or exceed typical presentations in terms of FIND criteria.

CHAPTER 2

Causes and Consequences of Pediatric Bipolar Spectrum Disorder

Ian, 13-year-old boy in middle school, was brought in to see a psychologist by his parents. The referral was initiated as his family was becoming increasingly concerned about his deteriorating level of functioning. While his grades showed a gradual decline over the past semester, dropping from A's and B's to primarily C's, his parents were especially distressed with the changes they were noticing at home. While they anticipated the adolescent years to be accompanied by specific challenges, Ian seemed to have changed fairly dramatically, alternating between very morose periods in which he withdrew, slept extensively, and focused on writing dark anime fan fiction, and, in stark contrast, other times when he seemed particularly energetic and "happy," but with a flavor that concerned them as it seemed pressured, artificial, and "giddy." He appeared irritable and edgy during both his more withdrawn periods and more energetic times, and this was a notable change from his preadolescent temperament, which had been fairly pleasant and easygoing, although "quirky" and "sensitive."

At the initial interview, Ian was cooperative and articulate, but seemed very shut down with a slow response time. He acknowledged passive suicidal ideation, and during subsequent individual time with the psychologist stated that he had relieved his emotional pressure by burning his skin superficially with a cigarette lighter. He stated that he felt very isolated at school, as he no longer thought he had anything in common with his previous friends, who "just don't really understand the existential angst of our position in the universe." Ian emphasized that he really didn't want to burden his family in any way, as "they are really good people," and stated "maybe they would be better off without me."

Home life is reportedly stable and both parents presented as warm, involved, and concerned about their son. However, they acknowledged that the family environment had become increasingly stressed and strained as they struggled with ways to cope effectively with Ian's erratic periods. Ian lives with his father, a high school biology teacher, his mother, an assistant teacher in a local preschool center, and his 8-year-old sister. A review of the family history indicated that the father's family system had some members with attention-deficit/ hyperactivity disorder (ADHD). The mother had limited family medical history available, as she, herself, had been adopted at birth, but adoption records did note "mental illness" in Ian's biological maternal grandmother. The parents described some recent stressors, including the tragic death of Ian's paternal uncle in a car accident and financial strain as they were attempting to help care for the uncle's widow and her two small children.

Ian's case study illustrates the complexity of dynamics found within a comprehensive clinical framework. Holistic treatment of children and adolescents with Pediatric Bipolar Spectrum Disorder (PBSD) requires thorough conceptualization of a wide range of factors that contribute to illness presentation, severity, and outcome. This chapter reviews the etiology and course of PBSD through a biopsychosocial frame, which synthesizes the intricate interplay among these determinants.

Biopsychosocial Framework

The biopsychosocial model provides a comprehensive framework for integrating multiple causal and contributory factors for PBSD. According to this model, psychopathology is the result of intricate interactions between biological, psychological, and social influences. A practitioner completing an initial intake with Ian would review a wide range of: (1) *biological factors*, including genetic loading, overall health, neurobiological processing, and neurocognitive functioning; (2) *psychological factors*, including emotional regulation, personality variables, and behavior patterns; and (3) *socioenvironmental factors*, including cultural context, interpersonal relationships, and stressful life events. Each domain contributes both potential *risk* and potential *protective* influences, depending on the interplay of multiple complex dynamics. This integrated model of conceptualization can optimally inform diagnosis, prognosis, and ongoing treatment.

Biological Factors

Advances in neurological technology, including magnetic resonance imaging (MRI), functional MRI (f-MRI), and genetic mapping, are expanding our understanding of neurobiological factors implicated in PBSD. Strong and replicable data are emerging to confirm the significant role of genetics (Mahon, Burdick, and Malhotra 2015). One particular challenge in integrating biological research is that bipolar disorder (BD) is *polygenetic*, determined by a combination of genetic variants. Second, there is *phenotypic heterogeneity*, meaning that multiple underlying physiological factors can contribute to a single disorder. Third, *multifinality* dictates that a single risk factor may increase subsequent risk for multiple psychiatric disorders. Further, there may be *genetic subtypes* within BD, as individuals differ widely on multiple illness variables, including age of onset, predominant mood states, frequency of cycling, and level of recovery between episodes (Mahon, Burdick, and Malhotra 2015). For example, in a large familial risk study, Biederman et al. (2013a) found that when BD and ADHD were not comorbid with each other, pediatric BD-I and ADHD both "bred true" in families, as did BD-I comorbid with ADHD, suggesting a complex interplay of genetic loading.

Heritability and Genetics

Genetic heritability is the single greatest predictor of PBSD (Diler and Birmaher 2012). Family and twin studies have found very high heritability rates ranging from 59 to 87 percent (Benarous et al. 2016a). Risk for developing BD is increased sixfold for the offspring of a parent with BD, and nearly eightfold if a sibling has the disorder (Lichtenstein et al. 2009). Overall, as summarized by Youngstrom et al. (2012), the risk for developing PBSD is increased:

1. 5 to 10 times if a first-degree relative has the disorder
2. 2.5 to 5 times if a second-degree relative has the disorder
3. 2 times for "likely" or "indeterminant" BD in a relative (Youngstrom et al. 2012)

Adoption studies provide further evidence of the potency of genetic loading compared to environmental influences. Adopted children with a biological parent with BD have been found to have a fourfold risk for developing the disorder (Lichtenstein et al. 2009).

A positive family history is a particularly salient risk factor for *early onset* of BD. For example, a recent study found that among youth with BD-I and BD-II a higher proportion with onset prior to age 15 years had first-degree relatives with affective disorders, in contrast to those with later onset (Propper et al. 2015). Having *two* biologically related family members is an even greater risk factor, increasing the odds of developing PBSD 3.6 times (Birmaher et al. 2010). As shown in Figure 2.1, a large-scale international study of patients with BD-I found that the prevalence of diagnosed affective illness among first-degree relatives was strongly associated to age of BD onset (Baldessarini et al. 2012). Further, results showed that the rate of *childhood onset* was highest when a positive family loading for BD was present.

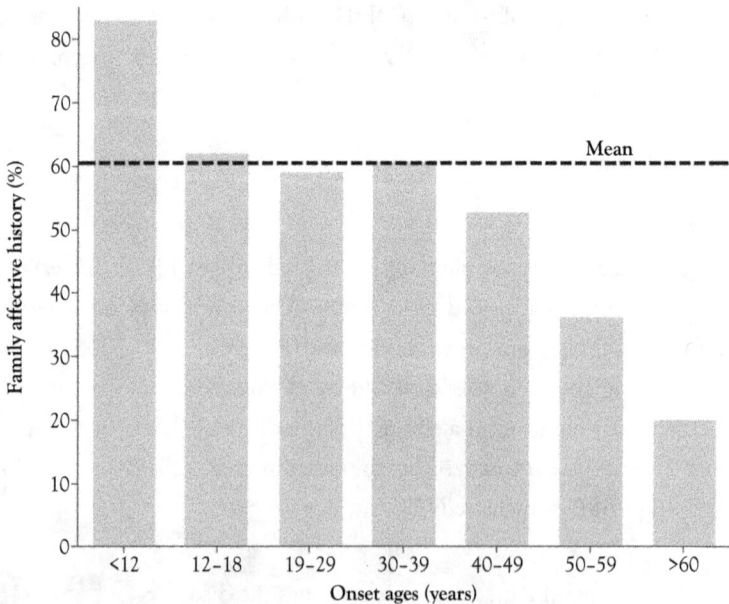

Figure 2.1 *Prevalence (%) of family history of affective illness versus onset ages among 1,665 Bipolar-I disorder patients*

Source: Reprinted from Baldessarini et al. (2012) World Psychiatry.

A review of studies to date indicates that biological propensity for PBSD is likely the result of numerous small polygenetic variables (Kennedy et al. 2015). A recent meta-analysis of genome-wide association studies identified 226 genes that are implicated in BD and multiple neurobiological pathways including: (1) hormonal regulation, (2) calcium channels, (3) second messenger systems, (4) glutamate signaling, and (5) neuronal development (Nurnberger et al. 2014). This is congruent with findings from a large, international retrospective study of outpatients with BD, indicating that parent and grandparent history of multiple psychiatric disorders, including but not limited to BD, was strongly linked to earlier age of onset (Post et al. 2016).

Age of Onset

Age of onset is consistently associated with more severe clinical trajectories, with worse outcomes reported for childhood-onset (prepubertal) in comparison to adolescent-onset BD (see Holtzman et al. 2015 for review). A recent meta-analytic review showed that early age of onset was associated with: (1) long treatment delays, (2) increased severity of depression, and (3) high levels of both comorbid anxiety and substance use, but *not* with increases in psychotic symptoms or mixed episodes (Joslyn et al. 2016). Propper et al. (2015) found that youth with onset prior to the age of 15 years were more likely than those with later onset to be characterized by: (1) an index episode of major depression, (2) a chronic clinical course, (3) rapid cycling, (4) comorbid ADHD, and (5) lower global functioning. Further, a study of an inpatient psychiatric sample of youth with BD reported that those with illness onset prior to the age of 13 years had more frequent rates of traumatic events, more first-degree relatives with BD, and higher rates of ADHD, in comparison to those with an onset after age 13 years (Goetz et al. 2015).

Figure 2.2 summarizes the distribution of age of onset in a large-scale international study of patients with BD-I (Baldessarini et al. 2012). Although peak prevalence was found within the adolescent to young adulthood years, onset of BD occurs across the lifespan. Further, there is accumulating evidence that PBSD can be identified as early as the preschool years, although accurate diagnosis may be challenging due to the

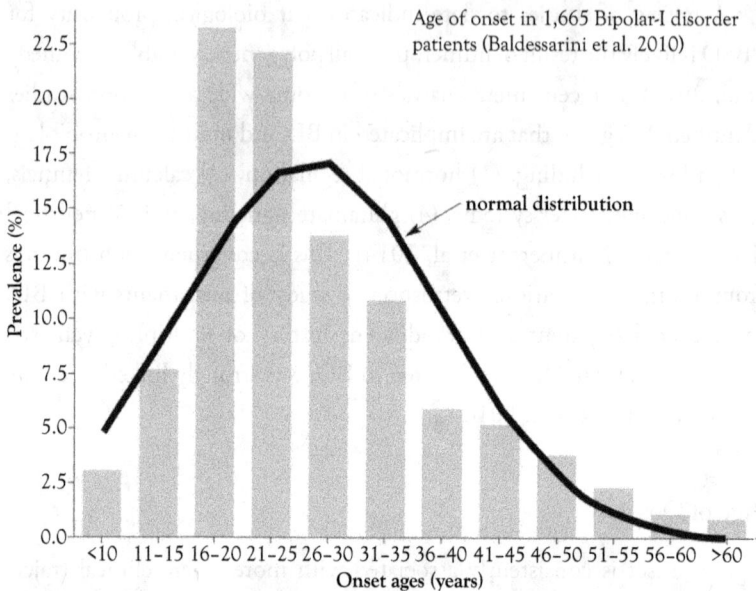

Figure 2.2 **Histogram of onset ages in 1,665 Bipolar-I disorder**
patients, with superimposed normal Gaussian distribution, indicating
moderate skewing toward younger ages

Source: Reprinted from Baldessarini et al. (2012) World Psychiatry.

very rapid cycling and mixed mood presentations which are typical in
these children, and must be made through a thoughtful developmental
lens (DeFilippis and Wagner 2015).

Gender

Equivalent rates of pediatric BD have been found for males and females,
paralleling adult gender distribution (APA 2013; Kessing, Vradi, and
Andersen 2015). In a large controlled study examining gender effects in
youth with BD-I, ages 6 to 17 years, both genders had highly impaired
interpersonal functioning, a wide range of emotional deficits, and similarly high rates of comorbid psychiatric conditions, including ADHD
and oppositional defiant disorder (ODD) (Wozniak et al. 2013).

There is emerging evidence, however, suggesting *differential presentations* of PBSD between the genders. For instance, in the BD-I sample
described earlier, in comparison to boys, girls had higher rates of panic

disorder and hypersexuality and a later age of onset of hypo/mania (Wozniak et al. 2013). Among youth who had been hospitalized for BD, boys had increased rates of neurodevelopmental lifetime disorders, including ADHD and learning disorders, while girls had higher rates of eating disorders and alcohol abuse (Goetz et al. 2015). Later age of treatment referral has also been found for girls in comparison to boys (Wozniak et al. 2013). Further, males are more likely to be *identified* for hypo/manic symptoms and females for depressive symptoms (Khazanov et al. 2015).

Medical Conditions

Prenatal issues including poor maternal health, prenatal malnutrition, and exposure to influenza during pregnancy, have been suggested as potential risk factors for the development of PBSD (Marangoni, Hernandez, and Faedda 2016; Youngstrom and Algorta 2014). Additionally, chronic infection has been linked to mood disorders, psychotic features, and suicidal behaviors. Specifically, toxoplasma gondji, an infection that is transmitted through cat urine, may be one such risk factor, as well as HIV, which could result in the development of manic symptoms (McNamara and Strawn 2015). Head injuries, within 5 years of first psychiatric admission, and seizures, may also increase the risk of developing PBSD, although more research is needed to confirm these associations (McNamara and Strawn 2015).

It is also important to note that differing medical conditions can mimic symptoms of PBSD. For instance, the following may manifest symptom presentations similar to mania: (1) temporal lobe epilepsy, (2) hyperthyroidism, (3) multiple sclerosis, (4) systemic lupus erythematosus, (5) alcohol-related neurodevelopmental disorder, and (6) Wilson's disease (see McNamara and Strawn 2015 for a detailed summary of non-heritable risk factors).

Lifestyle Health Habits

Sleep and Biorhythms.   Sleep disturbances are one of the first observable prodromal symptoms of PBSD, with *decreased need* for sleep being a diagnostic determinant, and sleep difficulties may persist even during periods of remission (Kim et al. 2014). Over 80 percent of children and adolescents with PBSD experience pervasive sleep problems, regardless of their BD subtype. Insomnia and reversal of circadian rhythms have been found to predominate during depressive episodes while *decreased need* for sleep characterize hypo/manic episodes (Baroni et al. 2012).

In a 2-year follow-up study of youth with PBSD, sleep disruption was significantly linked to both psychosocial and academic problems (Lunsford-Avery et al. 2012). Additionally, disrupted sleep patterns persisted in spite of participation in family focused treatment for adolescents, in which they were encouraged to regularize their sleep/wake cycles. Although sleep rhythm irregularity was associated with both manic and depressive symptoms, frequent night-time awakenings were linked only to depressive scores. This is congruent with findings on the long-term impact of sleep disturbances on symptom progression in adolescents with BD-I, as severity of depressive symptoms was predicted by increased numbers of awakenings and longer wake time on weekend nights (Gershon and Singh 2016).

Poor sleep quality has been linked to a variety of severe psychosocial consequences, including elevated levels of stress, emotional lability, impaired cognitive functioning, difficulties in academic performance, and both internalizing and externalizing symptoms (Heiler et al. 2011). Disruptions in daily routines and changes in circadian rhythms may also trigger manic features in adolescents with BD, especially if they have a tendency toward rapid-cycling mood symptoms (Diler and Birmaher 2012). Finally, circadian rhythms may be impacted by psychopharmacological regimens.

Nutrition.   Research is beginning to examine the impact of diet on PBSD. Micronutrients in foods, including vitamin D and omega-3 fatty acids, may be protective against the development of mood disorders (Youngstrom and Algorta 2014). Both vitamin and fatty acid deficiencies have been suggested as risk factors (McNamara and Strawn 2015). Youth with BD tend to have difficulty maintaining healthy nutritional habits, consuming fewer fruits and vegetables and more sugar and fat than is recommended in dietary guidelines (McNamara and Strawn 2015). Children and adolescents with PBSD may also struggle with weight issues, as they engage in emotional eating as an attempt at self-regulation. Finally, some medications used to treat PBSD, as indicated on Table 4.1 in Chapter 4, are associated with significant weight gain, which may negatively impact overall health as well as the youth's self-esteem and social status.

Neurobiological Markers

There is accumulating evidence of neurobiological abnormalities in the connectivity, shape, and function of various brain regions of youth with PBSD (Chang, Garrett, and Singh 2014). For instance, when compared to their typically developing counterparts (TDC), youth with PBSD have decreased connectivity between their amygdala and fusiform gyrus, which affects their judgment of facial expression of emotions (Rich, Fromm, and Berghorst 2008). Additionally, when compared to their TDCs, the faces that were remembered by youth with PBSD were encoded differently in the fusiform gyrus (Adleman, Kayser, and Olsavsky 2013). Table 2.1 summarizes key areas of the brain involved in the complex processes of PBSD. As noted, abnormalities in the structural development of these brain regions will contribute to dysfunction in multiple domains, including higher-order cognitive abilities, memory, and the processing of emotional stimuli (Diler and Birmaher 2012). White matter abnormalities and reduced corpus callosum volumes also impact hemispheric connections in youth with PBSD (Serafini et al. 2014). Toteja et al. (2015) found atypical age-associated alterations in the typical pattern of white matter development within the corpus callosum for bipolar patients, ages 9 to 62 years, suggesting differential maturation processes relative to typically developing peers.

Neuroanatomical abnormalities in the amygdala have been found to predict BD in children and adolescents with a relatively high specificity and sensitivity (Mwangi et al. 2014). Relative to TDCs, youth with BD-I have been shown to have *decreased connectivity* between the laterobasal subdivision of the amygdala, hippocampus and precentral gyrus, and *increased connectivity* between the laterobasal subdivision and the precuneus (Singh et al. 2015). Additionally, when youth with PBSD perceived fear through facial expressions, they showed hyperactivation of

Table 2.1 Brain regions impacted in youth with PBSD

Brain region	Disruptions in functioning in youth with PBSD
Left fusiform gyrus	-Processes facial perceptions -Decreased activation in youth with PBSD, causing difficulty in the utilization of visual cues to determine the mental and emotional state of others
Inferior frontal gyrus	-Linked with neural pathways involved in face and body recognition
Amygdala	-Emotion center located within the limbic system, linked to fear, anger, rage, and pleasure -Provides information to help determine if a stimulus is dangerous, and should be avoided, or can be approached -High incidence of smaller amygdala volumes in PBSD -Hyperactivity found in PBSD, even to a greater level than adult onset bipolar, which increases internal negative emotions -Disruptions can lead to mood dysregulation found in PBSD -Youth with PBSD experience lower amygdala laterobasal to prefrontal and hippocampal connectivity -Youth with PBSD show greater amygdala to precuneus connectivity
Prefrontal cortex (PFC)	-Responsible for executive functioning (EF) tasks including planning, considering long-term consequences, behavior inhibition, and overall cognitive and emotional control -Abnormal development appears to be a neurobiological risk factor for PBSD -Moderate evidence of smaller prefrontal volumes in youth with PBSD -Serving as a moderator, the PFC is unable to control the hyperactive amygdala, making it extremely difficult for youth with PBSD to regulate their emotions -Shares inhibitory connections with the amygdala and ventral striatum, which help inhibit nonadaptive behaviors -Hypoactive in youth with PBSD, especially during facial processing tasks -Regions of the PFC responsible for cognitive and emotional control are unable to moderate the overactive subcortical regions
Dorsolateral prefrontal cortex (DLPFC)	-Subsection of the PFC responsible for directing, shifting, and sustaining attention and higher (cognitive) mood regulation -Plays a role in regulating behavior inhibition and emotional regulation -Hypoactive in youth with PBSD, which can make the completion of attention and regulation tasks difficult

Ventrolateral prefrontal cortex (VLPFC)	-Subsection of the PFC responsible for regulating the peripheral nervous system, endocrine, and motor systems during stress -Essential for decision making, socio-emotional learning, and emotion regulation -Hypoactive in youth with PBSD, leading to the potential increase in behavioral and emotional arousal -Aberrant development may create the inability to control emotional responses and choose behaviors that are appropriate to the situation -Abnormal reward mechanisms, which reveal abnormal activation and connections in and from the VLPFC, may be an early marker for the risk of PBSD
Ventromedial prefrontal cortex (VMPFC)	-Has dense and direct connections with the amygdala -Dysfunction may cause the inability to properly interpret the significance of affective stimuli, including social stimuli, for example, difficulty judging the meaning of an angry face
Subcortical and medial PFC	-Between these brain regions there is a loop responsible for affective evaluation -Youth with PBSD typically experience overactivity within this region, resulting in hypersensitivity and reactivity to negative emotions
Precuneus	-Linked with self-consciousness, episodic memory, visuospatial abilities, and theory of mind -Youth with PBSD may have an increased volume, leading to less efficient functioning

Source: Adapted from Perlman et al. (2013); Singh et al. (2015); Lee et al. (2014); Adleman et al. (2012); Diler and Birmaher (2012); Chang, Garrett, and Singh (2014); and Russo, de Zwarte, and Blumberg (2015).

the amygdala and reduced functional connectivity to other regions in the face-processing circuit (Rich et al. 2008).

Youth with PBSD experience disruptions within the development of the prefrontal cortex (PFC), amygdala, and ventral striatum. These neurological domains share substantial inhibitory connections that allow individuals to control maladaptive behaviors and modulate impulsivity (Russo, de Zwarte, and Blumberg 2015). As youth with PBSD develop, their PFC, and its executive functions, also passes through maturational stages. This systemic process can mask the neurocognitive deficits of BD into late adolescence and early adulthood (Russo, de Zwarte, and

Blumberg 2015). Practitioners who wish to go into more detail about these neurobiological structures may refer to the excellent review articles provided by: (1) Lee et al. (2014), (2) Chang, Garrett, and Singh (2014), and (3) Serafini et al. (2014).

Neurocognitive Processes and Implications

Neurocognitive and Intellectual Functioning. The relationship between intellectual ability and PBSD is complex, as the youth's performance on cognitive measures will likely be impacted by: (1) neurobiological changes linked to the onset and course of BD, (2) severity of symptom presentation at the time cognitive functioning is assessed, and (3) medication-related effects. These issues are illustrated in Case Study 5, which provides scores from intellectual assessments across the span of 10 years. Assessment scores obtained during acute illness stages, particularly during psychiatric hospitalization, should be interpreted within the context of the youth's high levels of dysregulation.

Youth with PBSD typically present with intact intellectual abilities within the average range, although their performance on IQ measures may be impacted by particular areas of cognitive deficits. Systematic reviews indicate that children and adolescents with PBSD show specific neurocognitive impairments relative to TDCs, congruent with differential neurobiological process detailed previously (see Frías et al. 2014b; McCarthy et al. 2016). In sum, deficits are often found in: (1) working memory, (2) processing speed, (3) verbal memory, and (4) visual-spatial memory (Frias et al. 2014b, Nieto and Castellans 2011; Wozniak et al. 2013). In contrast, verbal fluency, visual memory, and visual-motor skills appear relatively affected (Nieto and Castellans 2011; Lera-Miguel et al. 2015).

The degree of cognitive impairment experienced by youth with PBSD appears to be moderated both by disorder subtype and by illness severity, particularly the presence of psychotic symptoms. In a sample of youth with pediatric-onset BD, Schenkel et al. (2012) found that those with BD-I scored significantly lower than TDCs across cognitive domains, including attention, executive function, working memory, visual memory, and verbal learning. In contrast, youth with BD-II scored similarly to typically developing peers on all measures except for verbal learning and memory, and performed *better* than their peers with BD-I on all domains, with the exception of working memory. Within an inpatient sample of adolescents hospitalized with BD, severity of mood disorder, and, specifically, the presence of current psychotic features, was associated with lower IQ and with greater working memory deficits, but did not specifically impact processing speed (McCarthy et al. 2016). Similarly, the presence of psychotic symptoms in adolescents with BD-I or II was linked to poorer development of executive control across a 2-year follow-up (Lera-Miguel et al. 2015).

The presence of comorbid diagnoses may further complicate the association between intellectual abilities and PBSD. A systematic review indicates that ADHD comorbidity may be linked to greater impairment in verbal memory and executive functioning (EF), but does not appear to impact sustained attention or processing speed (see Frías et al. 2014a). In sum, neurocognitive deficits appear more greatly impacted by the severity of the mood disorder, in contrast to the presence of a comorbid diagnosis.

Finally, specific domains of cognitive functioning may be differentially responsive to psychopharmacotherapy. For example, in an early-onset sample of youth with PBSD, both processing speed and visual-motor skills normalized during a 2-year pharmacotherapy period, whereas EF, working memory, and verbal and visual memory remained impaired, in comparison to typically developing peers (Lera-Miguel et al. 2015). Similarly, significant improvement in cognitive abilities, linked with mood stabilization, was found for youth with PBSD treated with lamotrigine over a 14-week period; both working memory and verbal memory showed marked gains, while deficits in both executive function and attention persisted relative to TDCs (Pavuluri et al. 2010).

Global Intellectual Abilities.   Premorbidly, a higher childhood IQ score, and especially high verbal abilities, may be a marker for risk of subsequent onset of BD. A positive association between IQ, as assessed at age 8 years, and lifetime manic symptoms at age 22 to 23 years was reported within a large birth cohort study for full-scale IQ, and both verbal and performance IQ subscales, with the strongest link reported for verbal IQ

(Smith et al. 2015). Additionally, specific symptom presentation may differentially impact domains of cognitive performance. For example, a dimensional study of manic symptoms in adolescents found that *exuberance* (characterized by high energy and cheerfulness) was associated with higher verbal IQ, while *undercontrol* (characterized by distractibility, irritability, and risk-taking behaviors) was associated with poor response inhibition (Stringaris et al. 2014).

A gender-specific pattern was found for IQ presentation in a study of youth with BD-I (Wozniak et al. 2013). Although youth with BD-I had a full-scale IQ within the normal range, comparable to TDCs, they scored lower on digit symbol, oral arithmetic, and digit span subscales. For boys, but not girls, BD-I was associated with a lower full-scale IQ and a lower vocabulary subscale score.

Executive Functioning (EF): Youth with PBSD often have challenges with the complex process of EF, which is an "umbrella" skill set including the domains of: (1) inhibition, (2) working memory, (3) planning, (4) set-shifting, and (5) fluency (Walshaw et al. 2010; Frías et al. 2014b). Particular problems have been noted for response inhibition, which may contribute to impulsive and risky decisions for youth with PBSD (see Frías et al. 2014b). EF deficits seem to persist over time, even with pharmacotherapy, indicating a slower rate of cognitive maturation within this domain for youth with PBSD (Lera-Miguel et al. 2015). Urosevic et al. (2016) recently reported that in comparison to typically developing peers, those with PBSD did not show age-related improvement in delay tolerance, the tendency to prefer immediate rewards over delayed reward opportunities; further, greater delay discounting was associated with current hypo/manic symptoms. EF impairments appear more impacted by severity of illness presentation, particularly a history of psychosis, rather than by comorbid ADHD symptoms per se. Udal et al. (2013) found that a history of psychotic symptoms for youth with PBSD was associated with impairments in cognitive flexibility, working memory, interference control, and processing speed, while youth without psychosis only showed deficits on processing speed. In sum, children and adolescents with PBSD often have difficulties planning, processing in a logical, sequential order, predicting outcomes, and effectively integrating information to achieve an end goal (Frías et al. 2014b). These deficits create multiple academic and social struggles.

Attention: A review of the research indicates that the *selective attention* of youth with PBSD is similar to that of typically developing peers, although they may have difficulty with *sustained attention*, particularly for emotionally valenced information (Dickstein et al. 2016; Frías et al. 2014b). Somewhat surprisingly, the presence of comorbid ADHD does not appear to increase sustained attention deficits, although in contrast to youth with BD-II, those with BD-I do more poorly within this domain (see Frías et al. 2014a).

Memory: Memory ability is often impaired in PBSD, including visual-spatial memory, working memory, and verbal memory (Schenkel et al. 2012; Wegbreit et al. 2016). Further, children and adolescents with a history of psychotic symptoms appear to have particularly marked memory problems, including recognition, recall, and semantic clustering, which further inhibits their efficient coding of verbal material (Udal et al. 2013; McCarthy et al. 2016). Visual memory, however, appears to remain relatively intact (Nieto and Castellanos 2011).

Cognitive Flexibility: Youth with PBSD demonstrate challenges with cognitive flexibility, which impact their ability to adapt to changes in environmental expectations and respond effectively to feedback (Udal et al. 2013; Walshaw et al. 2010). Severity of symptoms appears to specifically impact cognitive flexibility, as youth with BD-I or BD-II, in comparison to those with other spectrum diagnoses, have marked difficulty with reversal-learning tasks, which require the ability to modify attention in response to changing task goals (Dickstein et al. 2016). Further, impaired cognitive flexibility in youth with BD-I may be independent from other EF deficits, overall intelligence, and comorbid diagnostic status, including ADHD (Wegbreit et al. 2016). Lack of flexibility may contribute to frustration and emotional outbursts characteristic of children and adolescents with PBSD, as they struggle to generate novel problem-solving strategies, inhibit new behaviors, and adapt to shifting task demands.

Processing Speed: The processing speed of children and adolescents with PBSD has been found to be slower than that of typically developing peers (Udal et al. 2013), but comparable to that of peers with major depression (McCarthy et al. 2016). Additionally, decreased processing speed may have a disruptive effect on the ability of the youth with PBSD to process emotionally valenced words, regardless of the subtype of the disorder (Dickstein et al. 2016; Frías et al. 2014b).

Academic Performance and Educational Achievement.   The educational performance of youth with PBSD is impacted by both neurocognitive factors and mood dysregulation, which negatively affects the child and adolescent's ability to adapt within the academic environment, independent of their intellectual capabilities. For example, in a 4-year longitudinal study of youth with early-onset BD-I, Wozniak et al. (2013) found the large majority had received some academic support. There was a differential pattern of educational services for gender: (1) 92 percent of girls and 89 percent of boys had received some extra help, (2) 22 percent of girls and 42 percent of boys had been in a specialized class, and (3) 8 percent of girls and 16 percent of boys had repeated a grade. In comparing youth with BD to either those with unipolar depression or TDCs, Lagace and Kutcher (2005) found that only 58 percent of youth with BD graduated on time from high school, in contrast to 85 percent of those with unipolar depression and 92 percent of TDCs; further, these youth had high rates of specific mathematics difficulties, likely linked to slower response times.

Research to date suggests that either very high or very low premorbid school achievement may serve as a risk marker for the subsequent onset of BD (MacCabe et al. 2010). A prospective whole-population cohort study of all children in the Swedish national school register found that excellent scholastic performance at age 16 years conferred a nearly fourfold increased risk of psychiatric hospitalization for bipolar symptoms, in comparison to average performance, while students with the poorest grades were also at moderately increased risk for BD (MacCabe et al. 2010). This pattern was particularly marked for boys. These data parallel results from the prospective study of the Dunedin Cohort, as the small number of youth in this population sample who later developed mania had significantly higher IQs than other cohort members (Koenen et al. 2009). These findings are congruent with biographical studies noting associations found between BD and linguistic and musical creativity, which may be particularly linked to enhanced expansiveness, energy, and increases in goal-directed activity that characterize hypo/manic episodes (Goodwin and Jamison 2007).

Psychological Factors

The psychological presentation of children and adolescents with PBSD has been discussed extensively in Chapter 1, as these factors are core to diagnostic status. In summary, PBSD encompasses a broad range of psychological symptom presentations, and an in-depth exploration of these symptoms can be found in Table 1.3 within Chapter 1. However, dynamic developmental changes in emotional processing, personality, and behavioral manifestations described in the following sections will provide a more comprehensive examination of how these factors further impact psychological functioning.

Emotional Perception and Regulation

Emotional dysregulation is a core feature across diagnostic BD categories and current mood states. The episodic affective disruption that characterizes PBSD is marked by intense fluctuations, including irritability, rage, sadness, and elevated and expansive mood. Youth with PBSD not only struggle to moderate their own extreme internal emotions, but they also struggle to accurately interpret emotions expressed by others. The ability to accurately process emotions is impacted by neurological deficits described earlier (see Table 2.1) (Russo et al. 2015).

Children and adolescents with PBSD experience marked challenges in identifying emotionally laden information from nonverbal social cues, including the ability to accurately identify facial expressions and discriminate the emotional tone of verbal statements (Deveney et al. 2012, Wegbreit et al. 2015). Research indicates that these youth struggle to use facial cues to identify and interpret both negative and positively valenced emotions, although they may be particularly predisposed to misinterpret benign facial expressions as sad, angry, or hostile (Diler et al. 2013; Perlman et al. 2013). Additionally, deficits have been found in children and adolescents with BD-I, but not BD-II, in the ability to integrate verbally-mediated social and contextual cues to understand the mental states of others, regardless of the emotional valence of the information (Schenkel, Chamberlain, and Towne 2014).

Diler et al. (2013) found that that during depressive episodes, youth with BD-I and II showed increased attention to ambiguous facial expressions, but decreased attention to positive facial expressions, suggesting that present mood state may further interfere with emotional processing abilities. However, difficulties with emotional perception may not be confined to current mood dysregulation, as youth ages 7 to 17 years with either BD-I or BD-II made significantly more total errors on emotional labeling for child, but not adult faces, than did TDCs, even when they were primarily euthymic (Seymour et al. 2013). Impaired emotional perception is also impacted by deficits in information processing. For example, youth with BD-I demonstrated a negative attribution bias, as they endorsed and recalled more negative than positive words, a processing error that persisted at follow-up (Whitney et al. 2012).

Healthy social interactions for youth with PBSD may be impeded both by difficulties in identifying emotional facial expressions as well as in recognizing emotional prosody in spoken language (Siegel et al. 2015a). Additionally, these youth are predisposed to fixate on the presence of negative emotions, and lack the cognitive flexibility to redirect their attention, which can further exacerbate disinhibited and impulsive responses (Diler and Birmaher 2012). In sum, multiple deficits in emotional processing contribute to ongoing interpersonal deficits in the formation and maintenance of healthy social relationships (Chang et al. 2014).

Temperament and Personality

Heightened emotionality as a temperament trait has been associated with increased risk of psychopathology, particularly mood disorders, in offspring of parents with BD (Doucette et al. 2013). Many youth with PBSD have low frustration tolerance, become easily upset in challenging situations, and are highly emotionally reactive when given negative feedback (Rich et al. 2010). High levels of emotional arousal and reactivity, particularly negatively valenced affect and irritability, may be linked both to illness presentation and to more stable personality constructs. For example, preschoolers at high risk for PBSD due to positive family history show more irritability and inflexibility, as indexed by more intense anger dysregulation and pervasive noncompliance relative to TDCs (Tseng et al. 2015).

Research on personality styles of youth with PBSD is limited, as personality is a fluid construct that is forming and changing throughout developmental maturation. One study, however, looked at borderline personality traits in transitional aged youth, ages ranging from 16 to 24 years (Yen et al. 2015). Greater symptom severity and a worse prognosis, including higher risk for suicidality, were found when BD was comorbid with borderline personality features (Yen et al. 2015). In order to avoid misdiagnosis, it is important to distinguish the chronic emotional instability and impulsivity of borderline personality features from episodic mood changes that mark BD, although the two presentations may co-occur (APA 2013).

Behavioral Dysregulations

Dysregulated behaviors are a cardinal symptom of PBSD, and have been linked to neurological irregularities, which hinder the ability to inhibit maladaptive behavior patterns (Russo et al. 2015). Impulsivity and lack of adequate behavioral control may increase the involvement of youth with PBSD in high-risk activities, particularly during the adolescent years.

The behavioral activation system (BAS) and behavioral inhibition system (BIS) are motivational systems found to underlie mood disorders in youth (Gruber et al. 2013). The *BAS Dysregulation Hypothesis* suggests that PBSD involves a tendency toward extremely high or low levels of BAS activity (see Youngstrom and Algorta 2014). High BAS is linked to expected reinforcement, reward, and increased positive affect, which is associated with hypo/mania. In contrast, low activation of the BAS is associated with anticipating a lack of reward, energy loss, and decreased positive affect, all factors commonly found in depression (Hanmaker, Grasman, and Henk Kamphuis 2016). High-risk adolescents with high levels of reward sensitivity at baseline were more than three times as likely as those with moderate sensitivities to develop first onset of BD over a 1-year follow-up period (Alloy et al. 2012). The BIS triggers sensitivity to cues of threat, which aligns with the high levels of anxiety often associated with PBSD (Alloy et al. 2012; Gruber et al. 2013).

The integrated reward and circadian rhythm dysregulation model proposes that vulnerability to bipolar spectrum disorders is increased by a *combination* of reward hypersensitivity associated with high BAS *and* disruptions in social circadian rhythms (Alloy, Nusslock, and Boland 2015). Dysregulated daily activity schedules are likely to disrupt circadian rhythms, creating greater vulnerability for PBSD. Congruent with this two factor model, over the course of a 2-year follow-up period, social rhythm irregularity predicted greater likelihood of first onset of BD in high-reward sensitive adolescents, but not for their peers with moderate reward sensitivity (Alloy et al. 2015). These findings provide additional support for Interpersonal and Social Rhythm Therapy as an intervention for youth with PBSD, as discussed in Chapter 4 (Goldstein et al. 2014).

Increased risk for suicidality common in youth with PBSD has been previously discussed in detail in Chapter 1. High rates of self-harm (69.3 percent), suicidal ideation (73.9 percent), and suicide attempts (36.4 percent) have been found across BD subtypes (Hirneth et al. 2015), and across developmental stages (Weinstein et al. 2015). Higher suicidality in youth with PBSD is associated with greater cognitive vulnerability, including low self-esteem and hopelessness, and with emotional vulnerability, including more pronounced depression and poorer quality of life (Weinstein et al. 2015).

Esposito-Smythers et al. (2010) found that both children (ages 7–11 years) and adolescents (ages 12–17 years) reported relatively high rates of nonsuicidal self-injury (NSSI) both during their most current mood episode (both 22 percent) and across lifetime (both approximately 35 percent), with NSSI being associated with severity of depressive symptoms. Although there were no age effects for frequency of NSSI, age-related differences were found in clinical correlates. Among children, NSSI was associated with a diagnosis of either BD-I or II (versus NOS), psychosis, separation anxiety disorder, and greater severity of depressive symptoms. Among adolescents, NSSI was linked to mixed mood episodes, suicide attempts, and poor psychosocial functioning (Esposito-Smythers et al. 2010).

Social and Environmental Factors

A broad array of social and environmental factors contribute to both the development and trajectory of PBSD. Multiple contextual variables embedded within the interpersonal world of the youth with PBSD have the potential to serve as either risk or protective factors.

Cultural Context

The cultural context inhabited by a child or adolescent can impact both their exposure to and utilization of professional services and treatment inhabits. For instance, The Cross-National Collaborative Group study found lower rates of BD in Asian countries, which was attributed to increased focus on somatization rather than on specific mental health concerns (Merikangas et al. 2011). Therefore, professionals working with diverse individuals should be sensitive to cultural underpinnings that can impact the interpretation, understanding, and acceptance of PBSD. Culturally-based factors that may impact diagnosis and treatment include: (1) clinician lack of awareness of multicultural variables, (2) differences in distress thresholds across diversity groups, and (3) variations in the expression and reporting of mental illness across diverse racial and ethnic groups (for a review, see Liang et al. 2016).

Race and Ethnicity

As discussed in Chapter 1, research indicates that the prevalence of BD is equally distributed among ethnic groups (APA 2013; Van Meter et al. 2011). Previously reported differences were most likely due to: (1) confounding SES factors, (2) diversity variables in describing and reporting symptoms, and (3) potential clinician bias.

For example, African-American youth are more likely to be diagnosed with psychotic features, in particular auditory hallucinations, whereas their European-American counterparts typically are diagnosed with delusions (Khazanov et al. 2015). Racially-linked variations have also been found in diagnostic and disposition patterns shown in psychiatric emergency services. For instance, African-American youth are more likely to be diagnosed with behavioral and psychotic disorders; Hispanic or Latinos are more likely to receive disruptive-behavior disorders or substance-use disorders; and European-Americans are more likely to be diagnosed with major depression and alcohol-use disorders (Muroff et al. 2008). Additionally, European-American youth are more likely to be prescribed medications, particularly mood stabilizers and atypical antipsychotics, than their peers from other ethnic backgrounds (Kowatch et al. 2013). Therefore, care must be taken to minimize diagnostic biases as this may have detrimental effects on treatment, course, and outcome.

As a clinical practitioner, it is important to also keep in mind that patients from ethnically diverse backgrounds may be less inclined to seek formal mental health services until the severity of symptomatology surpasses their ability to function. As a result, these individuals are more likely to have severe symptom presentations at initial treatment contact (Muroff et al. 2008). Additionally, minority youth have been found to receive less mental health services than their European-American counterparts (Liang, Matheson, and Douglas 2016). Therefore, it is important to be aware of the racial and ethnic factors that contribute to treatment patterns and overall outcomes of youth with PBSD. For example, in the National Comorbidity Study (Khazanov et al. 2015), non-Hispanic Black teenagers with BD received less treatment for copresenting psychological concerns than did Hispanic or non-Hispanic White youth.

Socioeconomic Status

Although PBSD presents equally across SES groups, socioeconomic contexts may influence other environmental variables including access to nutrition, exposure to violence and trauma, availability of mental health services, and ability to obtain medical care (Youngstrom and Algorta 2014). These variables, in turn, can impact course and outcome in youth with PBSD. Among children and adolescents with PBSD, lower SES was found to contribute overall to a worse illness course (Birmaher et al. 2009), while higher SES moderated effects of depression severity (Birmaher et al. 2014).

A study by Schoeyen et al. (2011) found that individuals with BD had equivalent levels of education, when compared to TDCs, but significantly lower social and occupational functioning. In addition, they had higher rates of being single, household incomes below the poverty line, and were more likely to be on disability pension. These demographics highlight the importance of early identification and intervention in order to help children and adolescents with PBSD maximize their long-term functioning, and achieve their long-range potential.

Interpersonal Relationships

The initiation and maintenance of adaptive interpersonal relationships is a profound challenge for many children and adolescents with BDs (Schenkel et al. 2014). The social competence of youth with PBSD is negatively impacted by emotional dysregulation, which creates negativity and irritability within their social relationships and also interferes with their ability to effectively process interpersonal cues (Benarous et al. 2016b). Underlying deficits in EF and increased intensity of emotional arousal further impair youth's ability to effectively navigate their social world. Adaptive social interactions are also compromised by the difficulties children and adolescents with PBSD experience in identifying emotional facial expressions and in recognizing emotional prosody in spoken language (Siegel et al. 2015a). Furthermore, impairments within peer and familial relationships predict a worse course trajectory for these youth (Keenan-Miller et al. 2012).

Disruptions in positive social-learning opportunities may incrementally impact interpersonal difficulties throughout the lifespan (Keenan-Miller and Miklowitz 2011). Compromised social and emotional functioning contributes to a continued decrease in social satisfaction, lack of support, reciprocity, and relational trust (Siegel et al. 2015b).

Peer Relationships.   Chronic and extreme dysregulation, inaccurate interpretations of social interactions, and corresponding maladaptive responses expressed by youth with PBSD contribute to ongoing interpersonal discord and disruptions, including peer rejection (Keenan-Miller et al. 2012; Peters, Henry, and West 2015; Siegel et al. 2015b). Difficulties with peer relationships have specifically been found for children and adolescents with manic symptoms, even when subsyndromal (Benarous et al. 2016b), and youth with BD-I evidence particularly profound social cognitive deficits (Schenkel et al. 2014). While these deficits intensify during mood episodes, the impairments still exist at mild to moderate levels even during times when mood is stabilized, further impeding the ability to initiate and maintain friendships (Keenan-Miller et al. 2012).

However, dimensions of manic symptoms may be differentially associated with social competence. Recent research in a large community-based study found that overall, youth with manic symptoms had lower parent-reported interpersonal competence compared to typically developing peers; however, those with *predominantly exuberant manic symptoms* scored *higher* on social aptitude relative to TDCs, whereas those with *primarily undercontrolled manic symptoms* had *lower* social aptitude scores, both by parent and self-report (Benarous et al. 2016b).

Family Relationships.   The family environment of children and adolescents with PBSD plays an important role in shaping their clinical and developmental trajectory, and is often characterized by high levels of chronic family stress and conflict (Fristad et al. 2012; Klaus, Algorta, Young, and Fristad 2015). Many studies have focused on the quality of family relationships of youth with PBSD. A large outpatient study of 6- to 12-year olds with PBSD found higher levels of parent-reported family stress, which distinguished children with PBSD from those with other diagnoses (Fristad et al. 2012). Finally, among youth with PBSD, family rigidity is linked to increased suicidal ideation (Weinstein et al. 2015).

Research has found that increased conflict and the expression of negative emotions in a family system is associated with an earlier age of onset, faster recurrence of mood episodes, and poorer response to treatment in pediatric samples of PBSD (Sullivan et al. 2012; Nader et al. 2013). As previously discussed, BD is highly heritable; therefore youth with PBSD have an increased likelihood that their parent(s) also have BD, or another mood disorder, which predicts increased severity of the child's manic and depressive symptoms (Peters et al. 2015). Parental psychopathology may reduce parental engagement, monitoring, and control of household structure, which consequently, can exacerbate any underlying genetic factors. Family members' experience with their own mood disorder likely compounds familial stress, and may exert intergenerational influence. For example, Belardinelli et al. (2008) found that within families of children with PBSD, the presence of a mood disorder in a first- *or* second-degree relative was associated with lower levels of cohesion and family organization.

Emotional dysregulation between parent and child can also increase the threat of abuse, which is another risk factor for developing PBSD (Youngstrom and Algorta 2014). In contrast, self-esteem, psychological stability, and a strong support system, either in the home or through peer and nonparental adults, can serve as protective factors significantly moderating the course of the illness (Goetz et al. 2015). Additionally, the parent's utilization of their own support systems can create a protective factor counteracting the negative impact their symptomatology can create (Peters et al. 2015).

The reciprocal interplay of parent and youth communication dynamics creates a bidirectional cycle of negative affect and heightened emotional reactivity within the family system (Nader et al. 2013). For instance, to reduce potential damage and danger generated by BD symptoms, high levels of parental control and vigilance may be needed. Additionally, youth with BD require parenting abilities that far exceed a typical skill set. The cumulative strain of raising a child with PBSD is reflected in findings from a 4-year longitudinal study of BD-I from childhood into midadolescence, which indicated that youth with a persistent bipolar course initially had high family cohesion scores, but reported greater family conflict at the time of follow-up (Wozniak et al. 2011). Due to the arduous task of providing necessary care, there is the heightened probability of tension between adult caregivers, which then has the potential to create hostility, irritability, and avoidance within the family sphere (Siegel et al. 2015b).

The quality of the family environment may be differentially impacted by specific symptom presentations. A recent cross-sectional study of teenagers with PBSD found that manic symptoms and emotional dysregulation were associated with high levels of both adolescent- and parent-reported conflict (Timmins et al. 2016). In addition, comorbid externalizing symptoms were related to parent-reported conflict, while adolescent-reported family conflict was negatively correlated with SES and lifetime psychiatric hospitalization. Higher depression scores for adolescents with BD have been longitudinally linked to low family cohesion and adaptability (Sullivan et al. 2012), while parents of youth with PBSD with an "ill but improving" course endorsed more family conflict than did parents of youth with either "predominantly" or "moderately" euthymic trajectories (Birmaher et al. 2014).

Research investigating the emotional atmosphere of families using expressed emotion (EE) found that high levels of EE, which reflect criticism, hostility, or emotional overinvolvement toward a psychiatrically ill family member, were linked to a more severe illness outcome across multiple mental disorders, including BD (Nader et al. 2013). Within families of youth with PBSD, EE is also associated with greater length of depressive episodes, higher relapse rates, greater frequency of suicidal ideation, and higher numbers of manic and depressive symptoms at follow-up (Belardinelli et al. 2008; Ellis et al. 2014). Negative parental EE at baseline predicts poorer clinical outcomes at follow-up, both for youth with PBSD and those at high-risk for PBSD, as indexed by longer time to recovery, greater symptom severity, and global impairment (Klaus et al. 2015; Miklowitz et al. 2013; Sullivan et al. 2012).

Additionally, the quality of the family environment has implications for the effectiveness of treatment, particularly the outcome of family-based interventions, as discussed in Chapter 4. Overall, a more positive and supportive family atmosphere appears to potentiate the effects of interventions. However, there is some evidence that family-based treatment effects may be more positive for youth from families who initially had higher rates of conflict (Fristad and Macpherson 2014; Miklowitz et al. 2013). However, EE did not impact treatment response in multifamily treatment programs for children with PBSD (Macpherson et al. 2014).

Stressful Life Events

There is a wide body of research demonstrating the negative effects of childhood adversity on physical and psychiatric health. Youth with PBSD endorse an increased frequency of stressful life events when compared to peers with nonbipolar diagnoses (Fristad et al. 2012). Negative life events including trauma, the death of a parent or close family member, neglect, and even bullying are frequently seen in the histories of youth with very-early-onset PBSD (Goetz et al. 2015). Stress within the family system, as discussed previously, may also affect the progression of PBSD, especially during the early stages (Goetz et al. 2015). Furthermore, accumulated traumatic events may contribute to an earlier age of onset in youth who possess a genetic predisposition for BD (Anand et al. 2015).

Physical or sexual abuse or both are common within PBSD, especially in children aged 6 years and younger, and particularly if they have a comorbidity with post-traumatic stress disorder (PTSD), psychosis, or conduct disorder (Bernstein and Pataki 2015). Rates of physical and sexual abuse for youth with PBSD are higher than for the general population (Maniglio 2013b), although they may be similar to rates for youth with other psychiatric disorders (Rocher Schudlich et al. 2015). Further, youth with PBSD are more likely to report a *combination* of both physical and sexual maltreatment than youth with other clinical diagnoses, and their abuse history is associated with greater psychiatric comorbidity, including suicidality (Rocher Schudlich et al. 2015). Additionally, a recent retrospective study documents the adverse effects of verbal abuse, which was reported by almost 60 percent of respondents with BD, and was related to an earlier age of illness onset, rapid cycling, and increased rates of comorbid anxiety and substance abuse (Post et al. 2015). While verbal abuse frequently occurs within the context of physical and sexual abuse, its presence alone was associated with significantly early age of onset, while the combined presence of verbal, physical and sexual abuse further decreased onset age.

Overall, abuse is associated with differences in both the timing and course of PBSD (Maniglio 2013a), and is linked to more severe and complex clinical presentations (Maniglio et al. 2013b; Rocher Schudlich et al. 2015). A recent meta-analysis of 30 studies found more negative clinical features and a more severe course of illness in patients with BD who had experienced childhood maltreatment, including physical, sexual, or emotional abuse, neglect, or family conflict (Agnew-Blais and Danese 2016). Compared to individuals with BD, and no history of childhood maltreatment, those with childhood abuse or adversity experienced: (1) earlier age of BD onset, (2) higher rates of rapid cycling, (3) more severe manic, depressive, and psychotic symptoms, (4) more frequent manic and depressive episodes, and (5) greater risk for suicide attempts (Agnew-Blais and Danese 2016). Further, individuals with BD and a history of maltreatment had higher rates of comorbidity and dual diagnoses than those with no abuse history (Agnew-Blais and Danese 2016). The pivotal contribution of environmental adversity is highlighted by recent findings from a national sample of youth in Brazil, which indicated differentially high rates of PBSD for youth living in the most disadvantaged region of the country, which is marked by violence, substance use, and poverty (Rolim-Neto et al. 2015).

In contrast, protective factors for youth with BPSD can positively impact the course and outcome of this disorder. These protective factors include academic achievement, social competence, the presence of a supportive and consistent caregiver, and an adaptive response to stressors (Roberts, Bishop, and Rooney 2008). Additionally, it has been found that strong cognitive ability, warmth and consistency in parenting, positive family communications (i.e., Fristad et al. 2009), and high self-esteem (Weinstein et al. 2015) serve as protective factors for individuals with BD.

Complex Interplay Among Risk and Protective Factors

In sum, there is a complex interplay between biological vulnerabilities and environmental factors, including psychosocial stressors. This dynamic interaction is reflected in recent results from the ongoing Course and Outcome of Bipolar Illness in Youth (COBY) study (Birmaher et al. 2014). A latent class growth analysis of the 8-year clinical course of youth ages 7 to 17 years who had been diagnosed with PBSD identified four groups: (1) "predominantly euthymic" during most of the follow-up period (24 percent), (2) "predominantly ill" (22.3 percent), (3) "moderately euthymic" (34.6 percent), and (4) "ill with improving course" (19.1 percent). In comparison to the "predominantly ill" group, the "predominantly euthymic" youth had: (1) later symptom onset, (2) lower frequencies of self-injurious or suicidal behaviors, and (3) lower rates of comorbid ADHD and anxiety, linked to lower rates of medication with stimulants and antidepressants. Factors that may have served a protective function for the "predominantly euthymic" group were lower rates of parental psychiatric disorder, lower rates of abuse, higher rates of intact families, and higher socioeconomic status, in comparison to the other groups. Finally, the effects of age-at-onset were stronger in youth with lower SES, while the impact of depression severity was absent among those with the highest SES (Birmaher et al. 2014).

A recent study found that although early-life trauma may impact age of onset directly through its role as an environmental risk factor, there are interaction effects with genotype that may advance or delay the age of illness onset (Anand et al. 2015). In this large retrospective study, an interaction with single nucleotide polymorphic gene variants and childhood trauma was linked to early age of BD onset (Anand et al. 2015). Further, psychosocial adversity experienced in childhood, including verbal, physical, and sexual abuse, also had a strong independent association with onset age. The combined presence of these two vulnerability factors at their highest level was linked to a very early average age of onset (5.9

years), while their absence was linked to the oldest (25.8 years) average age of onset (Post et al. 2016).

Finally, the "evolutionary-neurodevelopmental theory" (ENT) proposed by Ellis et al. (2011) suggests that the intricate combination of risk and protective factors experienced by youth with PBSD may actually have the potential to contribute to *enhanced* developmental trajectories, dependent on the dynamic interaction of genetic and psychosocial factors. ENT, based on theories of both biological sensitivity to context and differential susceptibility, proposes that individuals with heightened susceptibility to the environment display increased sensitivity to both negative and positive environments, as described by the "orchid" hypothesis. Thus, the neurobiological loading for heightened arousal and emotional reactivity experienced by children and adolescents with PBSD has the potential *within a supportive and responsive environmental context,* to actually enhance developmental outcomes. This interplay may explain, in part, the report of relatively high proportions of creative and artistic achievement cited among individuals with BD (Goodwin and Jamison 2007).

Practitioner Summary of Causes and Consequences of PBSD

1. The biopsychosocial model provides a comprehensive framework within which to integrate the multiple factors linked to onset and course of PBSD.
2. Although genetic loading is the strongest cause of PBSD, there is a complex interplay between biological factors and the youth's environmental context, clinically indicating multiple domains for intervention, particularly within the family and social sphere, as discussed in Chapter 4.
3. There is accumulating evidence of neurobiological abnormalities in the connectivity, shape, and function of various brain regions of youth with PBSD. The degree of cognitive impairment experienced by youth with PBSD appears to be moderated by disorder subtype and by illness severity, particularly the presence of psychotic symptoms.
4. Many youth with PBSD have low frustration tolerance, become easily upset in challenging situations, and are highly emotionally

reactive when given negative feedback. High levels of emotional arousal and reactivity may be linked both to illness presentation and to more stable personality constructs.

5. Awareness of both risk and protective factors can help the psychologist construct optimal treatment strategies, including: (a) decreasing risk factors that are open to modification, and (b) increasing protective factors through a strengths-based lens.

6. The "orchid hypothesis" provides a positive framework for helping both the practitioner and the family view the intense emotional reactivity of the youth with PBSD as a potential "gift."

CHAPTER 3

Evaluation and Assessment Framework

The erratic mood and behavior fluctuations inherent in pediatric bipolar spectrum disorders (PBSD) create particular challenges for accurate assessment, similar to making a movie reel over time, as opposed to taking a single snapshot. The episodic nature of PBSD increases the possibility of misdiagnosis; dependent upon illness course, the youth may initially present as depressed or evidence high levels of externalizing symptoms. Conversely, clinicians may overestimate the likelihood of PBSD without adequate confirmation (Jenkins et al. 2011). When working with diverse populations, the practitioner needs to be particularly careful to interpret symptoms through a multicultural lens, as minority youth are particularly likely to receive misdiagnoses (Liang, Matheson, and Douglas 2016).

The critical importance of early identification of children and adolescents with PBSD is highlighted by the unacceptable lag between illness onset and intervention, with an average of 6 to 10 years of untreated illness (Jenkins et al. 2011). Misdiagnosis can lead not only to lack of treatment, but also to contraindicated treatment interventions, contributing to poor outcomes. The following case vignette illustrates the adverse impact of both inaccurate and delayed diagnosis on clinical trajectory.

McKenna was brought for an evaluation, due to her mother's referral from a friend whose son with PBSD had been effectively diagnosed and treated by the psychologist. At the time of the assessment, McKenna had an extensive treatment history, including residential placement and a "wilderness boot camp," with previous diagnoses of attention-deficit hyperactivity disorder (ADHD), oppositional defiant disorder (ODD), conduct disorder (CD), and depressive disorder. In spite of prior intervention attempts, her behavior had become increasingly unpredictable and risky, and she was currently facing legal charges due to a recent car theft. McKenna, who was then a few months away from her 18th birthday, was poorly motivated for the evaluation, but participated in the process, as this had been made a condition of returning to the family residence.

An extensive review of her symptom pattern, family history, and the addition of current psychological assessment, with both adolescent and parent report, gave a high likelihood of bipolar disorder (BD). In particular, McKenna showed an erratic mood, and periods of hypersexuality and decreased need for sleep. Unfortunately, she was very resistant to ongoing treatment, as previous psychosocial interventions had been primarily behavioral, which she viewed as punitive and pointless, or psychopharmacological, consisting of either a stimulant or antidepressant combination, both which she described as "making me feel quirky." Although the psychologist positively encouraged a new treatment approach based on the bipolar diagnosis, McKenna denied services, and as she shortly turned 18, the parents were unable to enforce follow-up.

Selection of comprehensive and specialized assessment tools should be made considering both the relative *sensitivity* and relative *specificity* of common symptoms of PBSD (see Table 1.4 in Chapter 1). *Sensitivity* improves the identification of youth with PBSD, while *specificity* contributes to the correct rule-out of non-PBSD syndromes, and together these dimensions can be combined to enhance the probability of an accurate diagnosis. To summarize, increased energy is the most sensitive symptom of PBSD, while elated, expansive mood, decreased need for sleep, hypersexuality, and emotional lability are highly specific symptoms.

The **FIND** criteria (Kowatch et al. 2009) is a "golden measuring rod" that can be used to distinguish specific PBSD mood symptoms from other common psychiatric disorders, as well as common variants of normative child and adolescent development.

1. **Frequency** of symptoms per week (symptoms most days of the week)
2. **Intensity** of mood symptoms
   a. Extreme disturbance in one domain
   b. Moderate disturbance in two or more domains
3. **Number** of symptoms per day (symptoms occur 3–4 or more times per day)
4. **Duration** of symptoms per day (≥4 hours per day, total, not necessarily contiguous)

Significant *clinical markers* that should lead to a more intensive evaluation of PBSD include the following (for additional information, see Youngstrom et al. 2012):

1. Positive family history of BD, with a first-degree relative indicating 5 to 10 times risk increase, and second-degree relative conveying a 2.5 to 5 times risk increase (Youngstrom, Freeman, and Jenkins 2009)
2. Marked *changes* in mood and behavior from the youth's typical developmental presentation, which are "outside age-appropriate norms"
3. Episodic mood lability
4. Episodic aggressive behavior, which seems reactive rather than planned
5. Early onset, atypical, or treatment-resistant depressive features
6. Antidepressant coincident mania, which may reflect previously undiagnosed PBSD
7. Decreased *need* for sleep
8. Psychotic features, as PBSD is a more common source of psychosis than schizophrenia (Tillman et al. 2008)

Comprehensive Developmental and Medical History

Within the context of a comprehensive assessment it is essential to obtain an in-depth exploration of the child's developmental history, family factors, and environmental context, as well as an evaluation of a broad range of clinical symptoms. An unstructured interview format, which includes both the youth and family members, can be very beneficial in providing a wide range of information, including: (a) prenatal and perinatal factors, (b) family mental and physical health history, and (c) details about social, emotional, and behavioral development. The importance of a lifespan evaluation of mood symptoms is highlighted by the fact that most self-referred treatment seeking occurs during depressive episodes, and without a minimal brief screening for hypo/mania, the youth may inadvertently receive a diagnosis of unipolar depression, based only on current mood presentation (Youngstrom, Freeman, and Jenkins 2009).

The Family History Screen (FHS, Weissman et al. 2000) is a brief instrument that can be used to assess psychiatric disorders among first-degree relatives. Data from the COBY study found that family history of hypo/

mania as indexed by the FHS was a powerful predictor of youth's transition from BD, unspecified, to BD-I and II (Axelson et al. 2011). Algorta et al. (2013) have recently validated the use of a short *Family Index of Risk for Mood issues* (FIRM, available free in Appendix A of their referenced article), which can easily be incorporated into a screening protocol. Scores on the FIRM, which summarize items endorsed for established BD risk factors, are interpreted as: (1) 0 to 2 "low risk," (2) 3 to 7 "moderate risk," and (3) ≥8 "high risk." FIRM scores effectively discriminate 5- to 18-year olds with PBSD from youth with all other diagnoses (Algorta et al. 2013).

There are multiple medical conditions which may "mimic" PBSD, and, as such, a thorough examination should be coordinated with the youth's pediatrician or family practitioner in order to screen for physical diseases, including infections, seizures, and metabolic disorders, such as thyroid imbalance. A comprehensive review is provided by McNamara and Strawn (2015). A salient example of the importance of the practitioner's review of medical factors is provided by the following vignette:

> *One of the authors had a fortuitous stroke of luck, having just attended a pediatric psychiatric conference, where the similarity between subcortical seizure disorder and BD was highlighted, immediately prior to conducting an initial evaluation on a middle-school boy. The patient presented with severe mood and behavioral dysregulation of a gradual onset within the past year, although there were no other specific risk factors indicating PBSD. As such, the psychologist requested that a full medical workup be conducted by the child's physician, including an electroencephalogram (EEG), based on conference research. Results indicated a complex seizure disorder, which responded very well to appropriate medication, and contributed to quick stabilization of the youth's erratic emotions and behaviors.*

Clinician-Administered Interviews

Diagnostic interviews provide a framework for assessing the severity of a broad range of clinical symptomatology, congruent with diagnostic systems, including the Diagnostic and Statistical Manual (DSM) and the International Classification of Diseases (ICD). The format of structured and semistructured interview tools has the potential to decrease possible intercultural biases, which may impact the practitioner's sound decision-making process. These interview formats provide comprehensive information, but their applicability to typical clinical settings may be limited due to time-extensive requirements. A review article by Galanter et al. (2012) provides more extensive information on the use of commonly utilized clinical diagnostic interviews with the evaluation of pediatric BD. Six interview scales applicable to PBSD are detailed below.

Bipolar Prodrome Symptom Interview and Scale-Prospective (BPSS-P)

The BPSS-P (Correll et al. 2014) is a clinician-administered interview specifically designed to identify emerging bipolar symptoms, and takes approximately two hours to complete. Among youth aged 12 to 23 years or their caregivers, the BPSS-P discriminates those with bipolar spectrum diagnoses from youth with depression-spectrum disorders and from typically developing counterparts (TDCs).

Child and Adolescent Psychiatric Assessment (CAPA)

The CAPA (Angold and Costello 2000) is a structured interview that assesses psychiatric symptoms over the past 3 months in youth ages 9 to 17 years, providing diagnoses for a range of clinical disorders, including mood disorders (Angold and Costello 2000). The most recent versions include both depressed affect and mania modules: (1) CAPA Child Interview Version 5.0 (Angold et al. 2008), and (2) CAPA Parent Interview Version 5.0 (Angold et al. 2008), and can be accessed at http://devepi.duhs.duke.edu/CAPA.html.

Development and Well-Being Assessment (DAWBA)

The DAWBA (Goodman et al. 2000) is a package of interviews, questionnaires and rating techniques designed to generate ICD and DSM psychiatric diagnoses for 5- to 17-year olds, and is the standard interview utilized in British surveys of child and adolescent mental health. It can be administered either by clinicians or through a computer format, and provides: (1) parent and teacher interview for ages 5 to 17 years, and (2) self-interviews for youth ages 11 to 17 years. The bipolar module can be accessed at http://dawba.info/Bipolar.

The Kiddie Schedule for Affective Disorders and Schizophrenia for School-Age Children—Present and Lifetime (K-SADS-PL)

A working draft of the K-SADS-PL (Axelson et al. 2009) is designed for ages 6 through 18 years and can be accessed online at: http://psychiatry. pitt.edu/research/tools-research/ksads-pl-2009-working-draft. The K-SADS-PL is available for free usage in both (a) clinical not-for-profit institutions and (b) IRB (institutional review board)-approved research protocols, with all other uses requiring the permission of the principal author, Dr. David Axelson.

Kiddie Schedule for Affective Disorders—Mania Rating Scale (K-SADS-MRS)

The K-SADS-MRS (Axelson et al. 2003) is a clinician-rated mania rating scale. It adopted 14 questions from the Kiddie Schedule for Affective Disorders and Schizophrenia for School-Age Children-Present Episode (K-SADS-P) 1986 version, plus a new item which assessed mood lability used to determine the presence of mania or hypomania during a period of time prescribed by the rater. At the end of the scale, the rater should note the onset and offset of the time period being rated.

The Washington University Schedule for Affective Disorders and Schizophrenia (WASH-U-KSADS)

The WASH-U-KSADS is specifically designed to assess for BD, including developmentally-specific symptoms and requires onset and offset points for all acknowledged symptoms (Geller et al. 1996). Specific sections on mania and rapid cycling are available (Geller et al. 2001).

Broad-Band Assessments

Diagnostically validated symptom rating scales and checklists are valuable tools for the clinician, due both to their low cost and ease of administration. Further, multiple checklists include youth self-report, parent, and teacher versions which can be incrementally helpful in providing a comprehensive view of the child or adolescent's clinical presentation across environmental domains. As summarized by Youngstrom, Freeman, and

Jenkins (2009), broad-band instruments can provide important diagnostic information for PBSD as:

a. high externalizing scores signal the possibility of PBSD, indicating further evaluation, particularly for hypo/mania,
b. low externalizing scores can decrease the likelihood of PBSD, and
c. indices of functional adaptability and impairment provide an index of clinical severity.

Although there are multiple broad-band instruments for children and adolescents, we have provided more detailed information below about three measures which may be particularly applicable to youth with bipolar spectrum disorders.

Achenbach System of Empirically Based Assessments (ASEBA)

The ASEBA (Achenbach 2009) is a comprehensive rating system that assesses both: (a) behavioral, emotional, and social problems, and (b) competencies, strengths, and adaptive functioning, with different age-based versions. Links to multiple ASEBA forms, resources, and bibliography are available at www.aseba.org. The ASEBA provides empirically derived indices of:

1. *Syndrome Scales*, including: (a) anxious/depressed, (b) withdrawn/depressed, (c) somatic complaints, (d) social problems, (e) thought problems, (f) attention problems, (g) rule-breaking behavior, and (h) aggressive behavior. These are combined through factor analysis to provide composite measures of internalizing, externalizing, and total scales.
2. *Competencies and Adaptive Scales*, including measures of: (a) activities, (b) social, and (c) school, which are combined to provide a competence composite.

For clarification of the following information, it should be noted that many studies to date are based upon the earlier version of the ASEBA system, in which the parent or caregiver report was the Child Behavior Checklist (CBCL)/4–18 spanning ages 4 to 18 years of age, including 20 competence items and 118 behavior problem items (Achenbach 1991a). This has been revised based on updated norms and is now designated the CBCL/6–18 spanning ages 6 to 18 years of age, and includes two additional behavioral items (Achenbach and Rescorla 2001). The Youth

Self-Report (YSR/11–18; Achenbach 1991b; Achenbach and Rescorla 2001) parallels the CBCL and is designed for ages 11 to 18 years. During revision, the same age range and same number of items were maintained, although some items were changed in content. The earlier version of the teacher's rating scale, the Teacher's Report Form (TRF/5-18; Achenbach, 1991c) has been revised as the TRF/6-18 (Achenbach and Rescorla 2001).

Child Behavior Checklist (CBCL)

To date, the CBCL (CBCL/4–19; Achenbach 1991a; CBCL/6–18; Achenbach and Rescorla 2001) is the most thoroughly researched broad-band assessment within the PBSD context, as studies indicate that youth with PBSD have elevated scores on multiple clinical syndrome scales, with the externalizing composite providing a highly sensitive indicator of PBSD (see Youngstrom et al. 2015). However, elevations on the CBCL externalizing composite are not diagnostically specific, as they reflect high levels of emotional and behavioral dysregulation across clinical diagnoses.

As such, they may be used as a screener indicating the need for additional focused evaluation. Several specialized PBSD profiles derived from the CBCL have been developed and are discussed as follows.

CBCL-JBD (Juvenile Bipolar Disorder) Profile or Severe Dysregulation Profile. The CBCL-JBD profile (also tagged "CBCL-PBD," Pediatric Bipolar Disorder) was proposed in response to findings suggesting that children and adolescents who had been diagnosed with PBSD had a distinct profile on the CBCL. The CBCL-JBD profile is defined by a pattern of T-scores above 70 on the anxious/depressed, aggression, and attention problems subscales (Faraone et al. 2005). A composite of 210 or over on these subscales has been suggested to maximize sensitivity and specificity of a current diagnosis of BD in comparison to ADHD (Biederman et al. 2009). Further, a positive CBCL-severe dysregulation profile has been found to identify a severe subgroup of BD-I youth, who present with earlier age of onset, higher rates of psychiatric hospitalization, and higher comorbidity rates of major depression, ODD, and anxiety disorders (Biederman et al. 2013b).

However, ongoing research indicates that the utility of the CBCL-JBD Profile is impacted by the child's age, diagnostic comorbidity, and current mood presentation, and may reflect more generalized behavioral dysregulation across disorders (Diler et al. 2009). A recent study that specifically evaluated the CBCL profile of unmedicated adolescents with BD-I, current episode depressed, found that although these youth had elevated scores on the CBCL-JBD, they did not reach designated clinical cut-offs; instead they scored above the clinical cut-off for the CBCL total and internalizing scores (Southammakosane et al. 2013). In a long-term follow-up of youth at high risk for mood disorders, due to maternal psychiatric history, the CBCL-PBD profiles (with cut-offs set at 60 to reflect an "at-risk" sample) were found predictive of ongoing comorbidity and impairment (Meyer et al. 2009). Across development, in contrast to youth without the CBCL-PBD profile, CBCL-PBD-profiled youth showed marked psychosocial impairment, increased rates of suicidality, and heightened risk for comorbid anxiety, BD, cluster B personality disorders and ADHD in adulthood, suggesting that this profile is predictive of severe impairment and broad-ranging psychiatric comorbidities rather than specific to PBSD. Together, these results indicate that the CBCL-JBD profile may be best interpreted as an index of symptom severity, functional impairment, and overall level of psychopathology, rather than specifically predicting PBSD. Current mood state may also impact the sensitivity of this index.

Child Behavior Checklist—Mania Scale (CBCL-MS). The CBCL-MS (Papachristou et al. 2013) corresponds to 19 items related to hypo/mania and psychosis. Scores above 70 mark a sixfold increase in PBSD risk, but do not differentiate between PBSD and ADHD on mean scores. In the TRAILS, a longitudinal, population-based study of over 2,000 adolescents, baseline scores for the CBCL-MS were significantly higher among youth who developed BD-I compared with scores of typically developing peers or those who presented with MDD or GAD on follow-up (Papachristou et al. 2013).

Behavioral Assessment System for Children, 3rd Edition (BASC-3)

The BASC-3 (Reynolds and Kamphaus 2015) is a multidimensional, multimethod rating scale that assesses behavior from three perspectives:

self, parent or caregiver, and teacher. It is available in both English and Spanish. The parent and teacher versions are designed for youth ages 2 to 21:11 years, and take approximately 10 to 20 minutes to complete. The self-report versions, Self-Report of Personality (SRP) span ages 6 to 25 years, and require approximately 30 minutes for completion.

Through the Parent Rating Scales (PRS) and Teacher Rating Scales (TRS), the BASC-3 provides empirically derived indices of:

1. *Clinical Scales*, including: (a) hyperactivity, (b) aggression, (c) conduct problems, (d) anxiety, (e) depression, (f) somatization, (g) attention problems, (h) learning problems, (i) atypicality and (j) withdrawal. These are combined through factor analysis to provide composite measures of externalizing, internalizing, and school problems, and a behavioral symptom index.
2. *Adaptive Skills Scale*, including: (a) adaptability, (b) social skills, (c) leadership, (d) study skills, and (e) functional communication.
3. *Content Scales*, including (a) anger control, (b) bullying, (c) developmental social disorders, (d) emotional self-control, (e) executive functioning, (f) negative emotionality, and (g) resiliency.

The SRP provides empirically derived indices of:

1. *Clinical Scales*, including: (a) attitude to school, (b) attitude to teachers, (c) sensation seeking, (d) atypicality, (e) locus of control, (f) social stress, (g) anxiety, (h) depression, (i) sense of inadequacy, (j) somatization, (k) attention problems, and (l) hyperactivity. These are combined through factor analysis to provide composite measures of school problems, internalizing problems, inattention/hyperactivity, and a behavioral symptom index.
2. *Personal Adjustment Scale*, including: (a) relations with parents, (b) interpersonal relations, (c) self-esteem, and (d) self-reliance.
3. *Content Scales*, including (a) test anxiety, (b) anger control, (c) mania, and (d) ego strength.

Although there is no research to date validating the use of the BASC-3 for PBSD, based on findings that externalizing scales from the Achenbach system are sensitive to the presence of BD (Youngstrom, Youngstrom, and Starr 2005), it is likely that two composite scales from the BASC-3 may also capture PBSD symptoms:

a. *Externalizing Problems* (hyperactivity and aggression)
b. *Behavior Symptom Index* (parent or teacher versions, including hyperactivity, aggression, depression, attention problems, atypicality, and withdrawal)

The most recent revision of the BASC-3 (Reynolds and Kamphaus 2015) has provided a Mania content scale for the Self-Report—Adolescent version (SR-A), described as "the tendency toward extended periods of heightened arousal, excessive activity and rapid idea generation." This is designed to help discern the presence of hypo/manic episodes, with possible differentiation from ADHD, but to date there is no predictive validity data available.

Child and Adolescent Symptom Inventory—5 (CASI-5)

The CASI-5 (Gadow and Spratkin 2015) assesses DSM-5 defined emotional and behavioral disorders, including depressive and manic symptoms, in youth ages 5 to 18 years.

For each symptom category there is an impairment question to index the extent to which symptoms impact youth's social or academic performance. The CASI-5 parent version includes 173 items, while the CASI-5 teacher version includes 125 items (Gadow and Spratkin 2015).

PBSD-Specific Inventories

Inventories designed specifically for assessment of PBSD focus on the presence of hypo/manic symptoms, as this is the symptom domain that differentiates PBSD from all other mood disorders. Table 3.1 provides a summary of PBSD-specific assessment instruments to be completed by a parent, caregiver, or other informed adult, while Table 3.2 summarizes self-report measures completed by the child or adolescent.

As seen in Tables 3.1 and 3.2, some instruments address only the presence of hypo/mania without mixed or depressive presentations, while

Table 3.1 Assessment instruments specific to PBSD completed by parent or informed adult

Instrument	Age	Description
CBCL-JPD or PBD (*Faraone et al.* 2005; *Meyer et al.* 2009)	6–18	-Scores > 70 on scales of aggression, attention/hyperactivity problems and anxiety or depression, for total > 210 -Modified in "high-risk samples" to > 60, providing 56 percent sensitivity, 88 percent specificity
Child Behavior Checklist-Mania Scale (CBCL-MS; *Papachristou et al.* 2013)	6–18	-19 items -33 percent sensitivity, 90 percent specificity -T-scores > 70 mark sixfold BD risk increase
Child Bipolar Questionnaire (CBQ; *Papolos et al.* 2006)	5–17	-65-item behavioral assessment tool -Likert scale format with responses ranging from 1–4 -Spanish version is available
Child Mania Rating Scale (CMRS; *Pavuluri et al.* 2006)	9–17	-21 items assessing mania, scored from 0 to 3 -Score greater than 20 indicates high likelihood of mania or hypomania -Available online as a parent screening tool at: http://dbsalliance.org/site/PageServer?pagename=education_screeningcenter_childmania -20 items teacher rating scale also available (CMRS-T)
Parent Mood Disorder Questionnaire (P-MDQ; *Wagner et al.* 2006)	12–17	-3 questions, Question 1 has 13 items, yes or no and Likert format -If checked 5 or more of the 13 behaviors on Question 1, marked "yes" on Question 2 and marked "moderate or serious" on Question 3, investigate a diagnosis of bipolar -72 percent sensitivity, 81 percent specificity -Available online at: http://bipolarnews.org/wp-content/uploads/2012/08/Mood-Disorder-Questionnaire-for-Parents-of-Adolescents.pdf
Parent Version, General Behavior Inventory (P-GBI; *Youngstrom et al.* 2001) • Hypomanic/biphasic scale • 10-Item Mania Scale (PGBI-10M)	5–17	-73 items, 4-point Likert-scale -Rates depressive, biphasic, hypomanic, and alternating mood symptoms -10 items, 4-point Likert-scale -Sensitive to treatment effects
Parent Version of the Young Mania Rating Scale (P-YMRS; *Gracious et al.* 2002)	5–17	-11 items -Scores range from 0–60 -Scores above 13 indicates potential mania or hypomania -Adapted from the YMRS (Young et al. 1978) -5 minutes to complete -Can be used by parent and teacher

Table 3.2 Assessment instruments specific to PBSD completed by child or adolescent

Instrument	Age	Time	Description
Adolescent General Behavior Inventory (A-GBI; Youngstrom et al. 2005)	12–17	15–20 minutes	-Self report completed by the adolescent -Adapted from GBI

Bipolar Spectrum Diagnostic Scale (BSDS; Ghaemi et al. 2005)	12+	5–10 minutes	-Essay format
			-Likelihood of PBSD
			  -0–6 highly unlikely
			  -7–12 low risk
			  -13–19 moderate risk
			  -20–25 high risk
			-Published cut-off score: 13
			-Optimal threshold for + diagnosis: ≥13
			-Sensitivity to BD-I and II: 75 percent
			-Specificity to unipolar depression: 93 percent
			-Available online at:
			http://psycheducation.org/diagnosis/the-bipolar-spectrum-diagnostic-scale/

Child Mania Rating Scale (CMRS; Pavuluri et al. 2006)	9–17	10–15 minutes	-21 items -Items rated on frequency per month -Items scored on a 4-point Likert scale -Useful in differentiating pediatric bipolar, ADHD, and no diagnosis
General Behavior Inventory-(GBI; Depue et al. 1989) General Behavior Inventory - Revised (GBI-R; Reichart et al. 2005) • *Depression* • *Hypomanic/Biphasic or mania*	13 +	40 minutes	-73 item self-report of hypomanic/biphasic and alternating mood symptoms -Cut-off score: 33 (22 items depression subscale and 11 items hypomanic or biphasic subscale) -Cut-off score: 21; sensitivity 89 percent, specificity 94 percent -Cut-off score: 5; sensitivity 78 percent, specificity 70 percent

(Continued)

Table 3.2 Assessment instruments specific to PBSD completed by child or adolescent   (Continued)

Instrument	Age	Time	Description
Hypomania Checklist (HCL-32; Holtmann et al. 2009)	15+	n/a	-32 self-report items -Distinguishes two main factors: (1) "active-elevated" hypomania, and (2) "risk-taking or irritable" hypomania -Discriminates between BD and MDD at sensitivity of 80 percent, specificity of 51 percent (Angst et al. 2005)
Jennie and Jeffrey Illustrated Interview for Children (Papolos, undated)	<12	15 minutes	-Picture format -Keyed to CBQ items
Mood Disorder Questionnaire (MDQ; Hirschfeld et al. 2000)	12+	5–10 minutes	-13 items -Cut-off score: 7 -Available in public domain at: http://www.dbsalliance.org/pdfs/MDQ.pdf
Mood Disorder Questionnaire-Adolescent Version (MDQ-A; Wagner et al. 2006; Miguez et al. 2013)	13–18	5–10 minutes	-15 items -Yes or no format -Cut-off score: 5 -38 percent sensitivity, 73 percent specificity -Designed for bipolar spectrum -Available in public domain
Young Mania Rating Scale (YMRS; Young et al. 1978)	5–17	15–30 minutes	-11 items -Items ranked on frequency during past 48 hours -Questions 1–4 rated 0 to 4 -Questions 5–9 rated 0 to 8 -Total scores range from 0–60

others more broadly evaluate mood symptoms, including hypo/mania. For diagnostic clarity, we suggest that one of the broader mood assessments be utilized as a primary screening, with those focused on hypo/mania incorporated to provide more specific and collaborative information.

In summary, to date, the most thoroughly validated instruments for PBSD include: (1) the CMRS (Pavuluri et al. 2006), (2) the P-GBI and its 10-item mania form (Youngstrom et al. 2001; Youngstrom et al. 2008), (3) the Mood Disorder Questionnaire-Parent (Wagner et al. 2006), and (4) the YMRS (Young et al. 1978; Frazier et al. 2007). However, ongoing research is providing additional information about the utility of other PBSD measures described in this chapter. It is important to note that the diagnostic accuracy of the test is directly influenced by the base rate of PBSD in the practitioner's setting. To supplement the detailed information available in Tables 3.1 and 3.2, the following section provides additional information on commonly utilized pediatric bipolar-specific assessment measures.

Child Mania Rating Scale (CMRS)

The CMRS (Pavuluri et al. 2006) is a 21-item screening instrument for mania, in which parents or caregivers rate items based on the youth's behavior and emotions in the past month. If the total of all items is more than 20, the child or adolescent should see a clinician for additional diagnostic evaluation as the rating indicates a high likelihood of current mania or hypomania.

General Behavior Inventories

General Behavior Inventory

The GBI (Depue et al. 1989) is a 73-item inventory designed to capture a comprehensive range of BD symptoms and their fluctuations over time. The GBI is currently free within the public domain (Dr. Depue requests notifications of use at rad5@cornell.edu). The 73 item self-report version of the GBI has been used with youth as young as 11 years old, but the length and the reading proficiency required for completion suggest that the modified versions listed below may be more appropriate for children and adolescents, particularly within typical clinical settings.

Parent-Report General Behavior Inventory. The P-GBI (Youngstrom et al. 2001) is an adaptation of the GBI from self-report to parent or caregiver report of the youth's mood symptoms, and includes two scales: depression and hypomanic/biphasic, with the hypomanic/biphasic scale having been shown better at discriminating PBSD (Youngstrom et al. 2001). The P-GBI is in public domain (the authors request information of how clinicians are using the instruments; contact Robert.Findling@uhhs.com or Dr. Young-strom at eay@unc.edu). As it is sensitive to intervention effects, it may also be used on an ongoing basis to monitor treatment progress.

Parent-General Behavior Inventory—10-Item Mania Scale (P-GBI-10M). The P-GBI-10M (Youngstrom et al. 2008) is a short form adapted from the GBI for use by parents of youth ages 5 to 17 years. Items are drawn exclusively from the hypomanic/biphasic scale of the GBI. The interpretation guide is as follows: 0 = Minimal, 1 to 4 = Mild, 5 to 14 = Neutral Risk, 15 to 17 = High, 18+ = Very High.

Adolescent General Behavior Inventory. The A-GBI (Danielson et al. 2003) parallels the P-GBI, modified to be utilized as a self-report assessment for adolescents and has been shown to discriminate well between youth with PBSD and those with other diagnoses.

The 7 Up 7 Down Inventory. The 7 Up 7 Down Inventory (Youngstrom et al. 2013) is a 14-item self-report measure of manic (7 items) and depressive (7 items) dispositions extracted from the GBI. It was designed and validated for ages 11 to 86 years of age in order to reflect BD symptom continuity from childhood and adolescence through adulthood (Youngstrom et al. 2013). Items for the 7 Up 7 Down Inventory are available in Appendix A, reproduced with permission from the author.

Mood Disorder Questionnaires

The MDQ (Hirschfeld et al. 2000) is a 15-item self-report measure of bipolar spectrum symptoms. It can be administered either by the clinician or self-administered by the patient. The first 13 questions address possible symptoms and are answered with either "yes" or "no." Two additional questions evaluate family history, past diagnoses, and disease severity. In order to assess bipolar symptoms in adolescents ages 12 to 17, it has been modified into the MDQ-P, to be completed by a parent or caregiver and the MDQ-A, the adolescent self-report (Wagner et al. 2006), containing 13 items. Although this measure can be completed by both the youth and the caregiver, better utility has been found when completed by the adult, with sensitivity at 72 percent and specificity at 81 percent (Wagner et al. 2006). The MDQ is better at screening for BD-I than for BD-II or other BD subtypes.

Young Mania Rating Scale

The YMRS (Young et al. 1978) is an 11-item, clinician-administered inventory, based on the patient's subjective report of his or her clinical condition over the past 48 hours. Additional information is based upon clinical observations made during the course of the clinical interview. It has practical clinical implications as it has been found sensitive to treatment effects. The P-YMRS (Gracious et al. 2002) is an 11-item questionnaire adapted from the YMRS, in which parents rate the severity of manic symptoms in their child over the past week, with higher ratings indicating more severe pathology.

Juvenile Bipolar Research Foundation Instruments

Child Bipolar Questionnaire

The CBQ (Papolos et al. 2006) includes the 65 highest ranked symptoms compiled from DSM criteria for mania, major depression and common comorbid disorders. The CBQ is self-administered by primary caregivers of youth ages 5 to 17 years, and results are reported in degrees of severity rather than categorically.

Jeannie and Jeffrey Illustrated Interview for Children (J/J)

The J/J (Papolos, undated) is designed as a companion assessment to the CBQ, to be administered to children with PBSD, and is delivered in a developmentally friendly format with pictures and case examples. The practitioner may want to incorporate this for supplemental information, although to date, we are not aware of any validation data.

Table 3.3 provides a reference of clinically significant benchmarks derived from commonly used checklists, which can be used to guide the practitioner in determining the need for more extensive assessment protocols.

Table 3.3 PBSD clinically significant change benchmarks from symptom checklists

Instrument	Away from clinical range	Back into clinical range	Closer to nonclinical
Benchmarks based on published norms			
Beck Depression Inventory *BDI mixed depression*	4	22	15
CBCL T-scores (2001 Norms) *Total* *Externalizing* *Internalizing* *Attention problems*	 49 49 n/a n/a	 70 70 70 66	 58 58 56 58
TRF T-scores (2001 Norms) *Total* *Externalizing* *Internalizing* *Attention problems*	 n/a n/a n/a n/a	 70 70 70 66	 57 56 55 57
YSR T-scores (2001 Norms) *Total* *Externalizing* *Internalizing*	 n/a n/a n/a	 70 70 70	 54 54 54
Benchmarks based on bipolar spectrum samples (Cooperberg 2004)			
YMRS	6	2	2
Child Depression Rating Scale-Revised	n/a	40	29
P-GBI *Hypomanic/Biphasic scale* *Depression scale*	 7 n/a	 19 18	 15 13
A-GBI *Hypomanic/Biphasic scale* *Depression scale*	 n/a n/a	 32 47	 19 27

Adapted from: Youngstrom et al. (2009). See original article for more detailed information on estimating probabilities of PBSD.

Other Assessment Instruments with Utility for PBSD

Measures of Depressive Symptoms

Although many of both the "broad-band" inventories and the PBSD-specific inventories described earlier contain separate scales for depression, practitioners may also administer a depression specific measure in order both to corroborate data supporting BD, and to assess more comprehensively for severity of depression symptoms and risk of suicidality. This is especially important considering that youth with PBSD: (1) often present initially with a depressive episode, (2) spend more of their dysregulated periods in depressed than hypo/manic mood states, and (3) are at particularly high risk for suicidality during depressive episodes in comparison to hypo/manic episodes (Diler and Birmaher 2012). The following details easily accessible measures that have clinical utility for both assessment and treatment monitoring of youth with PBSD.

Center for Epidemiological Studies Depression Scale Modified for Children (CES-DC)

The CES-DC (Faulstich et al. 1986) is a self-report inventory of 20 items rated on a 4-point scale, designed for ages 6 to 17 years. A cut-off point of 15 is indicative of significant levels of depressive symptoms, with a sensitivity of 71 percent and specificity of 57 percent for depressive disorders (Faulstich et al. 1986). This questionnaire can be accessed free online at: www.brightfutures.org/mentalhealth/pdf/professionals/bridges/ces_dc.pdf

Children's Depression Rating Scale-Revised (CDRS-R)

The CDRS-R (Poznanski, Freeman, and Mokros 1985) is a 17-item clinician-rated measure of depressive symptom severity, validated for ages 6 to 18 years, which is often combined with hypo/mania scales to more comprehensively assess the low mood and depressive features of youth with PBSD. It should be noted, however, that Frazier et al. (2007) found that within a PBSD sample, the CDRS-R had a pattern of decreasing diagnostic efficiency with increasing age, such that in the 14 to 17 age group, low scores indicated higher probability of BD, in contrast to high scores indicating higher probability in younger age groups.

Depression Self-Rating Scale (DSRS)

The DSRS (Birleson 1981) is an 18-item self-report measure for children and young adolescents, ages 8 to 14 years, and has been translated into 11 languages. Although the youth completes the scale, the clinician may read the statements out loud if the child has difficulty understanding the items. Items are scored 0 for "nondepressive" or normal responses, 1 for "sometimes" and two for "depressive" or abnormal responses. Research indicates a sensitivity of 66.7 percent and specificity of 76.7 percent for depressive disorders, and a cut-off score of 15 can be used to identify clinically significant depressive symptoms (Birleson et al. 1987).

Measures of Suicidality

Columbia Suicide Severity Rating Scale (C-SSRS)

The C-SSRS (Posner et al. 2011) is a semistructured clinician-administered rating scale for ages 6 years through the lifespan, which assesses both passive and active current suicidal ideation and suicidal behavior. Additional information may be accessed at www.cssrs.columbia.edu.

Suicidal Ideation Questionnaire (SIQ)

The SIQ (Reynolds 1988) is a self-report questionnaire for ages 12 to 18 years. It consists of 30 items for the SIQ (designed for 10–12th graders), with 15 items for the SIQ-JR (designed for 7–9th graders). This instrument assesses a wide range of suicidality, including ideation and intent. Significant suicidal ideation is indicated by scores above 40 for the SIQ and above 30 for the SIQ-JR (Reynolds 1988).

Functional Impairment and Quality of Life

Optimal management of PBSD targets both symptom reduction and the enhancement of overall functional adaptability. Each of the broad-band measures described earlier includes an index of either functional impairment or adaptive skills, which can be used on an ongoing basis to monitor quality of life. In addition, the Questionnaire for Measuring Health-Related Quality of Life in Children (KINDL; Ravens-Sieberer and Bullinger 2000) has been designed to assess quality of life with two parent and three youth report versions that are developmentally based and can be accessed free of charge (http://kindl.org/indexE.html). The KINDL is also available in multiple languages.

Relative Importance of Specific Respondent—Caregiver, Youth, Teacher

In a recent meta-analysis of rating scales for PBSD, symptom checklists were found to have discriminative validity for PBSD, with caregiver report emerging more strongly than reports generated by either youth or teachers, and this is particularly true for hypo/manic symptoms (Youngstrom et al. 2015). Clinically meaningful effect sizes using caregiver reports have been reported for: (1) the GBI, (2) MDQ, (3) CMRS, (4) ASEBA, and (5) CBQ. Both the MDQ and GBI were also found to be fairly effective as self-report measures for youth with PBSD. Superiority of parent rating in contrast to self-report has also found on the MDQ-A (Wagner et al. 2006).

A common guideline for children and adolescents is to increasingly weigh the validity of a youth's self-report with gains in developmental maturity, which are congruent with increases in meta-cognition and verbal proficiency. However, this guideline is modified for PBSD, as bipolar symptomatology often impairs the youth's insight, motivation and perspective, thereby compromising the accuracy of their self-report (Youngstrom et al. 2011). Caregivers have valuable ongoing information about changes over time in their child's emotional and behavioral patterns, and also spend more time consistently with them than do other adults; this may account for parent report being more informative than teacher report. Of note, the higher validity of parent report remains even when the parent has a diagnosed mood disorder themselves (Youngstrom et al. 2006). Freeman et al. (2011) found that caregivers notice irritable mood at significantly lower levels of mania than youth, while youth may more accurately self-report symptoms of increased energy, hypersexuality, and decreased need for sleep. Although teacher reports are valuable in providing additional validation across contexts and in comparing youth's presentation to that of peers, fluctuations in mood and energy are often not as readily observed within the classroom setting as at home. We would like to emphasize these findings, as many parents of PBSD youth find the information they provide is disregarded or minimized by professionals, as the child's emotional and behavioral dysregulation is often not as extreme when observed in structured contexts outside the family environment.

Factors Influencing the Usefulness of Assessment Instruments

Diversity Considerations

Although PBSD affects youth at similar rates across ethnic, cultural, and socioeconomic groups (See Chapter 2), the assessment instruments discussed in the current chapter have differential diversity utility, dependent on criteria samples. Although specific details are beyond the scope of this chapter, we strongly encourage the practitioner to be sophisticated about test selection for the individual patient and to maintain competency in assessment procedures through a multicultural lens. For current practice standards, refer to the Standards for Educational and Psychological Testing (American Educational Research Association, American Psychological Association, and the National Council on Measurement in Education 2014), which can be obtained through www.aera.net/ Standards14. Potential ethnic and racial discrepancies in diagnosis may be minimized through the use of structured diagnostic interviews and evidence-based algorithms for accurately interpreting risk factors and rating scales (Jenkins et al. 2011).

Overall, evidence-based assessment recommendations appear to remain relevant when generalized to new demographic groups and clinical settings (Jenkins et al. 2011; Pendergast et al. 2015). However, the culturally competent clinician will carefully consider diversity factors that contribute to diagnostic sensitivity and specificity. For example, in comparison to data from the original U.S. based validation study on the MDQ-A (Wagner et al. 2006), results from a Swiss sample showed higher sensitivity, particularly for adolescent self-report, but lower specificity for

BD (Miguez et al. 2013). Further, both the sensitivity and specificity of the CBQ within the Swiss study were lower than that reported in the U.S. validation sample (Papolos et al. 2006).

Clinical Context

In a recent review of self-rating instruments to identify young people, ages 15 to 25 years, at risk for bipolar spectrum disorders Waugh et al. (2014) found that optimal cut-off scores for sensitivity and specificity varied according to sample characteristics, including age and setting (non-clinical versus clinical). As such, the authors encourage practitioners to: (1) utilize optimal age-based cut-off scores, and (2) select at least two screening scales, one with high sensitivity and one with high specificity. The use of screening measures that have been found to be robust across diverse samples will further increase the accuracy of evaluation. Applicability across mental health settings can be enhanced by the clinician utilizing effective cut-off scores established within their specific population, as differential base rates of clinical settings directly impact the probability of PBSD diagnosis. Differences in symptom *severity levels* among community health settings, specialty clinics, and inpatient services will also impact the relative performance of the assessment tool.

Early Identification

Assessment tools that prospectively predict PBSD are especially needed for youth at high risk for developing BD, in order to close the gap between time of symptom onset and the initiation of treatment. The importance of early identification is highlighted by results from a recent meta-analysis (Van Meter et al. 2016b) showing that the prodrome period before an initial mood episode of BD lasts approximately 2 years, while the period of subthreshold symptoms preceding recurrent mood episodes averages one month. The ability to target early symptoms will enhance proactive treatment, which may, in turn, reduce illness severity over time. Ratheesh et al. (2015) have recently published a systematic review of relevant measures, suggesting that both the CBCL-PBD and the GBI may be particularly useful in prospectively predicting BD-I and BD-II in youth at risk.

Integration of Multiple Assessment Tools to Optimize Diagnosis and Treatment Planning

A summary of PBSD assessment and evaluation strategies to date indicates the superiority of utilizing multiple instruments from multiple informants. For example, both the YMRS and the K-SADS-MRS have shown excellent ability to separate PBSD from other clinical diagnoses among youth across ages 4 to 17 years, with each measure contributing unique variance to the prediction of bipolar illness (Frazier et al. 2007).

Sophisticated assessment of diagnosis will take into account base rates of PBSD in different clinical settings, which range from 1 percent in general medical outpatient practices, to 34 percent in acute psychiatric hospital settings (see Youngstrom, Freeman, and Jenkins 2009, Table 3.1). "Test-Wait" and "Test-Treat" thresholds can be used to decide what level of intervention to implement. "Test-Wait" thresholds indicate the need for continued assessment, which can be combined with psychotherapy focused on increasing a broad range of adaptive coping skills, stress management, and sleep hygiene, which may be protective against the future development of clinical symptoms as well as enhancing overall functioning, regardless of specific diagnostic status. In contrast, the "Test-Treat" threshold indicates a zone where probability is high enough to initiate treatment specific for PBSD (Youngstrom, Freeman, and Jenkins 2009).

More sophisticated and cost-effective identification of youth at risk for PBSD is needed in order to triage those at highest risk. Clinical practitioners can optimize diagnostic specificity with assessment strategies that are easily accessible, cost-effective, and combine multiple sources of information (Frazier et al. 2014). Bayesian techniques can be used to more accurately and efficiently diagnose PBSD by estimating the probability of BD based on clinical setting (i.e., outpatient recommended starting base rate is 6 percent), family history (i.e., odds of bipolar diagnosis increased by a factor of 2.5 for second-degree relative with BD), and a test score of 35 on the P-GBI (associated with a likelihood ratio of 2.3) (Jenkins et al. 2012). Youngstrom et al. (2012) present the benefits of using diagnostic likelihood ratios (DLRs) with a nomogram, a chart that yields Bayesian probabilities without requiring computations. This allows the practitioner to utilize an evidence-based decision making framework, including discriminately loading incremental risk factors.

Findings from the Longitudinal Assessment of Manic Symptoms (LAMS) sites, including children ages 6 through 12 years, indicate the utility of both logistic regression (Fristad et al. 2012) and classification tree algorithms (CTA; Fristad and Macpherson 2014) to improve the identification of youth with bipolar spectrum disorders. Both methods have utility for screening out youth with low probability of BD and identifying those for whom more intensive assessment is needed. In comparison to logistic regression, CTA appears to have increased sensitivity, with slightly decreased specificity and positive predictive power (Frazier et al. 2014). In particular, CTA indicated that high ratings of parent-reported mania on the PGBI-10M at both screening and baseline nearly doubled the PBSD probability. Additionally, low screening and high baseline PGBI-10M scores combined with positive parental history of mania almost doubled the probability of PBSD, indicating that several classification tree branches may be helpful in determining the presence of PBSD.

Practitioner Summary for Evidence-Based Framework for PBSD Assessment

In summary, practitioners can increase the accuracy of their diagnostic assessment and ongoing treatment evaluation by using the following steps:

1. Be aware of base rates of PBSD across different clinical settings.
2. Assess risk factors specific to PBSD. Refer to Table 1.1 in Chapter 1 for *sensitivity* and *specificity* symptoms.
3. Ensure that the child or adolescent has had a recent thorough medical check-up to screen for any physical or metabolic causes that may be triggering dysregulations.
4. Utilize multiple informant sources, including self-report, and parent and teacher report, keeping in mind that parental report is most likely to be accurate.
5. Administer a broad-band inventory to cover a wide range of clinical domains, assessing for PBSD, alternate primary diagnoses, and

comorbid diagnoses. As a guideline, on broad-band instruments, if the externalizing composite is highly elevated, odds of PBSD increase three- to fourfold (Youngstrom et al. 2012).

6. If there is a positive family history of BD and externalizing scores on broad-band measures are high, supplement the assessment battery with a PBSD specific measure.

7. Continue to carefully evaluate for suicide and self-harm risk.

8. Continue ongoing assessment of treatment progress, with modifications of intervention plan in response to changes in symptoms and functionality.

APPENDIX A

7-Up 7-Down Inventory

The 7 Up 7 Down Inventory
Following are some questions about behaviors that occur in the general population. Using the subsequent scale, select the number that best describes how often you experience these behaviors.

Item		Never or hardly ever	Sometimes	Often	Very often or almost constantly
1	Have you had periods of extreme happiness and intense energy lasting several days or more when you also felt much more anxious or tense (jittery, nervous, uptight) than usual (other than related to the menstrual cycle)?	0	1	2	3
2	Have there been times of several days or more when you were so sad that it was quite painful or you felt that you couldn't stand it?	0	1	2	3
3	Have there been times lasting several days or more when you felt you must have lots of excitement, and you actually did a lot of new or different things?	0	1	2	3
4	Have you had periods of extreme happiness and intense energy (clearly more than your usual self) when, for several days or more, it took you over an hour to get to sleep at night?	0	1	2	3
5	Have there been long periods in your life when you felt sad, depressed, or irritable most of the time?	0	1	2	3
6	Have you had periods of extreme happiness and high energy lasting several days or more when what you saw, heard, smelled, tasted, or touched seemed vivid or intense?	0	1	2	3
7	Have there been periods of several days or more when your thinking was so clear and quick that it was much better than most other people's?	0	1	2	3
8	Have there been times of a couple days or more when you felt that you were a very important person or that your abilities or talents were better than most other people's?	0	1	2	3
9	Have them been times when you have hated yourself or felt that you were stupid, ugly, unlovable, or useless?	0	1	2	3

		0	1	2	3
10	Have there been times of several days or more when you really got down on yourself and felt worthless?	0	1	2	3
11	Have you had periods when it seemed that the future was hopeless and things could not improve?	0	1	2	3
12	Have there been periods lasting several days or more when you were so down in the dumps that you thought you might never snap out of it?	0	1	2	3
13	Have you had times when your thoughts and ideas came so fast that you couldn't get them all out, or they came so quickly that others complained that they couldn't keep up with your ideas?	0	1	2	3
14	Have there been times when you have felt that you would be better off dead?	0	1	2	3

Source: Reprinted with permission of the author (Youngstrom et al. 2013). Please contact Dr. Youngstrom for suggested cut-off scores.

CHAPTER 4

Comprehensive Treatment

The complexity of Pediatric Bipolar Spectrum Disorders (PBSD) dictates that optimal treatment be multifaceted, combining psychotherapy, pharmacotherapy, and multisystemic supports. The most recent guidelines for treatment are available from the American Academy for Child and Adolescent Psychiatry (2007), and the National Institute for Health and Care Excellence (NICE 2016), and emphasize the importance of intensive, ongoing assessment and intervention in collaboration with family members. There is a growing body of evidence that supports the efficacy of both psychosocial treatments (Fristad and Macpherson 2014) and medication interventions (Diaz-Caneja et al. 2014) for children and adolescents with bipolar spectrum disorders.

The importance of early intervention and effective treatment strategies cannot be overemphasized. Long treatment delays between the onset of PBSD and first treatment contact are especially concerning, since earlier age of onset is associated with greater illness severity and higher rates of comorbidities (Diler and Birmaher 2012; McClellan, Kowatch, and Findling 2007). Untreated PBSD significantly interrupts the developmental trajectory of the child, as symptoms interfere with the ability to master pivotal cognitive, academic, social, and behavioral tasks. Longitudinal data underscore the importance of maximizing ongoing treatment, as even youth with fairly positive trajectories continue to experience syndromal and subsyndromal mood symptoms (Birmaher et al. 2014).

The following vignette illustrates many of these treatment challenges:

Xavier began outpatient treatment at the age of 7 years, as his mother was concerned about his increasingly erratic rages, which were typically followed by deep periods of tears, remorse, and self-recrimination. In addition to implementing multifaceted psychosocial strategies, the psychologist strongly recommended a psychiatric consultation, in light of both bilateral family loading for BD and Xavier's clinical presentation. However, his mother was initially reluctant to initiate a medication consultation, as a family member had tragically died of an adverse reaction to homeopathic remedies.

Intensive outpatient psychotherapy was initiated for 2 years, with an emphasis on emotional and behavioral regulation and psychoeducation. Some positive treatment progress was made, as both Xavier and his family were highly treatment compliant. However, as dysregulations persisted, the family eventually agreed to psychiatric consultation. A trial of an atypical antipsychotic was initiated, with slow, but incremental improvements in mood state and cognitive processing, which also facilitated psychosocial treatment response. With an ongoing combination of psychotherapy and pharmacological intervention, Xavier continued to consolidate gains in his emotional and behavioral control, friendship network, and educational progress. His improvement over the course of elementary school was so significant that upon graduation into middle school, he received the citizenship award for his class.

Discouragingly, many children and adolescents with PBSD do not obtain any form of mental health intervention, and even those entering treatment often receive inconsistent and periodic services (Khazanov et al. 2015; Vande Voort et al. 2016). Among youth with PBSD who do receive some form of intervention, up to 80 percent are initially treated for other psychiatric conditions, which clearly impedes optimal therapeutic response (Goetz et al. 2015). Recent results from a nationally representative sample of U.S. adolescents with BD-I or BD-II found that less than half were treated specifically for hypo/manic or depressive symptoms, while 13 percent received treatment for other mental health conditions, including attention-deficit/hyperactivity disorder (ADHD), oppositional defiant disorder (ODD), and conduct disorder (CD); unfortunately, 38 percent did not report treatment of any kind (Khazanov et al. 2015). Similarly, in a Danish nationwide sample, less than half of children and adolescents received an accurate diagnosis of PBSD at first professional contact, with nearly a year lapsing before BD diagnosis, while initial diagnoses included depressive disorders, psychotic disorders, and adjustment disorders (Kessing et al. 2015). This is particularly distressing in light of research emphasizing the importance of early intervention tailored to the specialized needs of youth with PBSD.

Even when economic and access barriers are removed, treatment follow-up may be variable. For example, within a federally funded integrated health system, less than half of children and adolescents with PBSD received psychotherapy after their initial diagnostic contact, in spite of the fact that almost 60 percent required psychiatric hospitalization during follow-up (Vande Voort et al. 2016). Of those with at least 6 months follow-up, 55 percent were treated solely by medication, with only 45 percent receiving the combination of pharmacotherapy and psychotherapy endorsed by clinical guidelines. Within clinical samples, treatment utilization has been found to increase with older age, greater symptom severity, suicidality, and the presence of comorbid psychiatric diagnoses (Khazanov et al. 2015; Shapiro et al. 2014). The presence of externalizing symptoms may particularly increase referral for intervention, as in a nationally representative U.S. sample, treatment was more common among bipolar youth with severe mood presentations and those with comorbid ADHD, behavior disorders (ODD or CD), and alcohol use (Khazanov et al. 2015).

Optimal treatment of PBSD entails collaborative interprofessional relationships among psychologists, psychiatrists, psychotherapists, behavioral and developmental pediatricians, social workers, and educational specialists in order to provide multifaceted interventions across domains of adaptive functioning. Practice parameters for pediatric bipolar disorder highlight the importance of multidisciplinary partnership, providing a combination of psychopharmacology and psychotherapeutic intervention as the "gold standard" for treatment (AACAP 2007; NICE 2016). The crucial importance of early intervention is emphasized by findings that the long-term trajectory of PBSD may be improved if effective treatment is established at, or near, initial symptom onset (Van Meter et al. 2016b).

Pharmacotherapy for PBSD

Table 4.1 presents medications currently approved by the Food and Drug Administration (FDA) for the treatment of pediatric bipolar disorder. In addition, other pharmacotherapies often used in PBSD treatment are listed, based on either their approved use for adult BD or for pediatric populations with other diagnoses. Detailed information on

Table 4.1 Psychopharmacotherapy interventions for pediatric bipolar spectrum disorder

Medication	Ages[1]	Considerations and possible side effects
Lithium** (Lithobid; Eskalith-CR)	12–17	-Narrow therapeutic index, requiring regular toxicity screens -May have neuroprotective effects -Side effects: Weight gain, insomnia, gastrointestinal upset, dizziness, polyuria, enuresis, tremor
Anticonvulsants		
Carbamazepine*[2] (Tegretol, Equetro)		-Rare possibility of Stevens-Johnson syndrome, aplastic anemia, and bone marrow suppression -Side effects: Sedation, dizziness, fatigue, vision difficulties, nausea, ataxia
Divalproex sodium*[2] (Depakote, Depakene)		-Caution in girls of child-bearing age as may lead to polycystic ovary syndrome (with hair growth and acne) and teratogenic effects -Side effects: Sedation, weight gain, gastrointestinal problems, tremor
Gabapentin[2] (Neurontin)		-Mild side-effect profile may include weight gain, sedation, dizziness, tremor
Lamotrigine*[2] (Lamictal)		-Rare risk of potentially-fatal Stephens-Johnson syndrome -Side effects: Sedation, gastrointestinal upset, headache, rash
Topiramate[2] (Topamax)		-Side effects: Weight loss, decreased appetite, sedation, gastrointestinal upset
Atypical antipsychotics		
Aripiprazole** (Abilify)	10–17	-May cause Parkinsonian symptoms -Low risk of weight gain -Side effects: Gastrointestinal symptoms, restlessness, sedation
Asenapine** (Saphris)	10–17	-Monitor dystonia -Side effects: Mild weight gain, sedation, dizziness
Clozapine (Clozaril)		-Considered primarily in treatment-resistant cases -Side effects: Weight gain, increased appetite, sedation, enuresis
Lurasidone (Latuda)		-Side effects: Nausea, restlessness
Olanzapine** (Zypreza)	13–17	-Possible changes in cholesterol levels and prolactin increases -Side effects: Weight gain, sedation

Quetiapine** (Seroquel)	10–17	-Possible changes in blood pressure -Side effects: Weight gain, sedation, gastrointestinal symptoms, headache
Risperidone** (Risperdal)	10–17	-Possible changes in cholesterol levels and prolactin increases -Side effects: Weight gain, sedation, extrapyramidal symptoms
Ziprasidone*		-Side effects: Sedation, fatigue, nausea, headache

Source: Adapted from Lytle, Moratschek, and Findling (2015) and Kowatch et al. (2009).
Note: Trade names are in parentheses.
** Medications approved by the FDA for PBSD, for which endorsed age ranges are provided
*FDA-approved for adult BD. [1]Ages are only provided for medications approved by the FDA for PBSD. [2]FDA-approved for pediatric seizure disorders.

pharmacological interventions can be obtained in several extensive review articles (Cox, Seri, and Cavanna 2014; Díaz-Caneja et al. 2014; Dorfman and Robb 2016). Ongoing updated information about medications for PBSD can be accessed at fda.gov.

Due to inherent implementation challenges in clinical research, many medication trials are limited to relatively short follow-up periods. Efficacy studies, to date, suggest lithium monotherapy or atypical antipsychotics as "first line of defense," with anticonvulsants recommended as second line or adjunctive therapies (Lytle, Moratschek, and Findling 2015). The FDA has recently approved asenapine (Saphris), as monotherapy for the acute treatment of manic or mixed episodes associated with bipolar I disorder in pediatric patients (www.accessdata.fda.gov/drugsatfda_docs/label/2017/022117s020s021lbl.pdf). Clinical trials of asenapine with youth with PBSD ages 10 to 17 years indicate a reduction of mania symptoms and overall illness severity in a 3-week study of treatment (Findling et al. 2015). However, at the time of press, only lithium and aripiprazole were FDA approved for *long-term treatment* of PBSD (www.fda.gov). Dorfman and Robb (2016) have recently published a review of long-term treatment strategies for pediatric bipolar disorder that indicates comparable effectiveness of second-generation antipsychotics and mood stabilizers in reducing manic symptoms. The authors stress the importance of maximizing early treatment benefits, due to variable rates of ongoing consistent medication compliance.

Medication compliance is a topic that should be thoroughly addressed through psychoeducation, as current clinical guidelines recommend 12 to

24 months of maintenance treatment, after remission of the first manic episode (Dorfman and Robb 2016). Further, ongoing pharmacotherapy is frequently indicated to prevent relapse and maximize adaptive functioning (McClellan et al. 2007). Youth face special challenges in maintaining multifaceted treatment compliance, due in part to continued stigma about mental health, emerging peer relationships with a desire not to seem different, and developing executive functioning skills. Modeling from other youth with PBSD may be especially helpful in maintaining ongoing treatment. For example, a teenager was able to encourage a middle school cohort by saying, "We need to take our princess pills so we don't turn into ogres." Participation in support groups may also be helpful to decrease stigma and increase motivation for sustained treatment.

It is common for children and adolescents to be treated with a combination of medications in order to address their complex PBSD symptom presentations. In addition, high rates of psychiatric comorbidity may require adjunctive treatment, secondary to mood stabilization (Lytle, Moratschek, and Findling 2015). Common supplementary pharmacotherapies include antidepressants and medications to address attention and concentration difficulties. Since many youth with PBSD have significant depressive periods, antidepressants, including the selective serotonin reuptake inhibitors (SSRIs, i.e., fluoxetine, sertraline) and bupropion, a norepinephrine-dopamine reuptake inhibitor (NDRI), are often used as adjunctives. However, there is some evidence that these may destabilize mood or induce a manic episode unless there is a "ground floor" medication for mood stabilization (Lytle, Moratschek, and Findling 2015). Bhowmik et al. (2014) found that children and adolescents with BD who received antidepressant monotherapy had a higher risk of a manic switch than those receiving second-generation antipsychotic monotherapy, highlighting the importance of cautious prescription of antidepressants in pediatric patients with bipolar depression. Further, there has been concern about the potential of antidepressants to increase suicidality, resulting in a "black box" warning from the FDA, although follow-up analysis indicates that even though a small sample of youth experienced increased suicidal ideation and behavior, there were no reported cases of completed suicide linked to fluoxetine treatment (Gibbons et al. 2012). Finally, we again emphasize the critical importance of accurate diagnosis in guiding treatment, as the selection of inappropriate medications has little potential

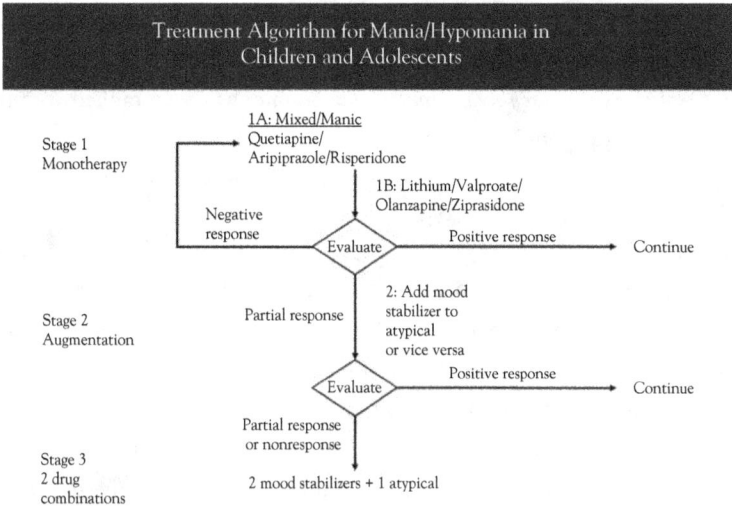

Treatment Algorithm for Mania/Hypomania in Children and Adolescents

Stage 1
Monotherapy

1A: Mixed/Manic
Quetiapine/
Aripiprazole/Risperidone

1B: Lithium/Valproate/
Olanzapine/Ziprasidone

Negative
response

Evaluate

Positive response → Continue

Stage 2
Augmentation

Partial response

2: Add mood
stabilizer to
atypical
or vice versa

Evaluate

Positive response → Continue

Partial response
or nonresponse

Stage 3
2 drug
combinations

2 mood stabilizers + 1 atypical

Figure 4.1 Medication treatment algorithm for children and adolescents with PBSD

Source: Kowatch RA et al. Clinical Manual for the Management of Bipolar Disorder in Children and Adolescents. Arlington, VA: American Psychiatric Publishing, Inc, 2008.

for benefits, while diagnostically contraindicated psychopharmacological treatment unnecessarily exposes youth to potential side effects and risks.

Figure 4.1 provides an algorithm that illustrates optimal stages of medication implementation.

Psychosocial Interventions for PBSD

Common goals of psychosocial interventions are: (1) symptom reduction, (2) psychoeducation, and (3) treatment adherence to promote positive developmental growth and prevent relapse (McClellan, Kowatch, and Findling 2007).

A summary of evidence-based psychosocial interventions for PBSD is provided in Table 4.2.

Division 53 of the American Psychological Association provides updated information about treatment options, which have been research-validated, through their website at www.effectivechildtherapy. org. To date, no psychosocial treatment has received the "well-established" ranking, which is based on large-scale randomized controlled trials by independent research teams. The following empirically-supported interventions are discussed in greater detail below:

Family psychoeducation plus skill building has received sufficient research
support to be designated as "probably efficacious."

Cognitive behavior therapy for bipolar disorder has been ranked "prom-
ising treatment."

Both *dialectical behavioral therapy* and *interpersonal and social rhythm
therapy* are currently "experimental."

While we strongly advocate the utilization of evidence-based treatment strategies, we also acknowledge some of the inherent difficulties for
many community-based or private practice clinicians in implementing
comprehensive treatment protocols designed within larger, research-based
institutions. Effective intervention is especially challenging for youth
in underserved and rural areas, as psychologists strive to meet multiple
needs with limited available resources. There is a growing literature base
indicating the effectiveness of modifying evidence-based therapy (EBT)
protocols through a modular approach, with an emphasis on maintaining
core treatment components (Bearman and Weisz 2015). Further, there
is a current interest in transdiagnostic treatment, an effective framework
that provides combined treatments that target common core symptoms
across PBSD and co-occurring disorders (Ehrenreich-May and Chu
2014). These modified treatment approaches provide a format for maintaining core therapeutic components from controlled evidence-based
studies, while maximizing the ability of the community-based practitioner to meet diverse clinical needs.

Across specific treatment protocols, integral components of effective
psychotherapy for youth with PBSD include:

1. Family based, including strong therapeutic alliance with the child or
   adolescent and family
2. Psychoeducation about PBSD
3. Monitoring of early warning signs and the development of a collaborative relapse prevention plan
4. Emotional regulation strategies, which include mood tracking
5. Stabilization of sleep cycles and social interactions
6. Skills building for family communication, social relationships, and
   problem solving
7. Careful consideration of developmental maturation of mood symptoms

Family-Focused Interventions

The importance of family-based interventions is highlighted by the family context of youth with PBSD. This often includes high levels of expressed emotion, negative life events, chronic stress, and low levels of family adaptability and cohesion, which are linked in part to the child or adolescent's challenging behavior (Keenan-Miller et al. 2012). Family-based treatments have the advantage of providing PBSD-specific techniques while also addressing these contextual factors which are linked to clinical outcomes as discussed in Chapter 3.

Psychoeducational Psychotherapy (PEP)

PEP can be delivered by both Individual Family Psychoeducation Groups (IF-PEP; Fristad, and Goldberg Arnold 2011a) and Multifamily Psychoeducation (MF-PEP; Fristad, and Goldberg Arnold 2011b) for youth with bipolar and depressive spectrum disorders. Treatment encompasses psychoeducation, family support, and skills-building based on cognitive-behavioral and family systems principles. As detailed at www.moody-childtherapy.com, the following intervention goals are highlighted for both IF-PEP and MF-PEP:

1. Increase knowledge and understanding of the mood disorder for all family members.
2. Differentiate the youth from his or her symptoms.
3. Incorporate biopsychosocial factors through a team-treatment approach.
4. Improve symptom management skills, with an emphasis of building a tool kit of coping strategies and making connections for *Thinking-Feeling-Doing*.
5. Enhance communication and problem-solving skills.
6. Increase the family's support and ability to access effective mental health services.

Randomized clinical trials indicate that PEP is associated with decreased mood impairment and behavioral symptoms in children, longer maintenance of treatment gains, enhanced family interactions, increased access to care, and more positive attitudes toward mental health services (Fristad et al. 2009). MF-PEP has also been shown to improve caregivers' knowledge of mood disorders (MacPherson, Leffler, and Fristad 2014).

The IF-PEP treatment protocol includes 20, 45- to 50-minute individual sessions, including manual-guided sessions, and 4 crisis management or additional practice sessions (Fristad and Goldberg-Arnold 2011a). The MF-PEP protocol incorporates 8, 90-minute sessions. As seen in the Resource section, the PEP treatment manuals and workbooks for children ages 7 to 18 years with bipolar spectrum and depressive disorders are available in both English and Spanish (Fristad and Goldberg Arnold 2011). These materials can be accessed at www.moodychildtherapy.com.

Although EBTs are typically developed within academic research centers, which have unique settings and resources, MF-PEP has recently been generalized to an outpatient community setting (MacPherson, Leffler, and Fristad 2014). This open treatment trial, which consisted of 8, 90-minute sessions, indicated the generalizability, feasibility and cost-effectiveness of this treatment protocol. Additionally, this research group is currently evaluating a video-conferencing version of IF-PEP via Tele-Health, which is accessible to rural children with mood disorders (www.moodychildtherapy.com).

Family-Focused Therapy (FFT)

Family Focused Therapy for Adolescents (FFT-A) is specifically designed to enhance the family's ability to cope positively with the disorder and to decrease criticism, expressed emotion, and conflict (Miklowitz et al. 2008; Miklowitz et al. 2009). This 21-session outpatient protocol for youth with bipolar spectrum disorder includes the patient, primary caregivers, and siblings, and is typically implemented adjunctively with pharmacotherapy. Primary intervention components encompass:

1. Psychoeducation, including symptom awareness, medication adherence, trigger identification, and relapse prevention
2. Family communication enhancement
3. Problem-solving skills training

The six core objectives of FFT-A are to (Miklowitz et al. 2012):

1. Integrate experiences associated with illness episodes.
2. Accept vulnerability to future episodes.
3. Embrace the role of psychopharmacotherapy in symptom management.
4. Distinguish between the youth's personality and bipolar symptoms.
5. Identify and cope effectively with stressful life events that may trigger mood dysfunctions.
6. Reestablish functional relationships after illness episodes.

Results from a 2-year randomized control trial of adolescents with bipolar spectrum disorders indicated that those who participated in FFT-A had improved speed and quality of recovery relative to those in "Enhanced Care" (three family sessions) (Miklowitz et al. 2008). Findings also highlighted the effectiveness of FFT-A for high-conflict families, as youth in initially high-EE (high-emotionally expressive) families showed more treatment responsiveness than those in low-EE (low-emotional expressive) families (Miklowitz et al. 2009).

Practitioners' resources for implementing FFT-A include:

1. *Clinicians' Treatment Manual for FFT for Early-Onset Youth and Young Adults (FFT-EOY)* (Miklowitz et al. 2012), which can be accessed through the Child and Adolescent Mood Disorders Program at www.semel.ucla.edu/champ/downloads-clinicians.
2. *Bipolar Disorder: A Family-Focused Treatment Approach*, 2nd ed. (Miklowitz 2010), available at Guilford Press.

FFT has been adapted for children and adolescents who are at high risk for developing bipolar disorder (FFT-HR), due to family history and affective symptoms (Miklowitz et al. 2013). As seen in Table 4.2, FFT-HR has a shorter treatment frame than FFT-A and has also been modified for school-aged children as well as teens. A randomized trial of FFT-HR with pharmacotherapy found that in comparison to a psychoeducation control group, FFT-HR participants had more rapid recovery from initial mood symptoms and more weeks in symptom remission across the 1-year study period (Miklowitz et al. 2013).

Table 4.2 Psychosocial interventions for pediatric bipolar disorder with clinical trials

Children		
Intervention	*Ages*	*Format and goals*
Child- and Family-Focused Cognitive Behavioral Therapy (CFF-CBT)** (West and Weinstein 2012; West et al. 2014)	7–13	-12 sessions, 6 booster sessions (18 total) -CBT with psychoeducation, social skills, family communication and problem-solving -Individual or multifamily group format
Psychoeducational Psychotherapy (PEP)** • Individual Family PEP (IF-PEP)** • Multifamily PEP (MF-PEP)** (Fristad et al. 2009; Fristad and Goldberg Arnold 2011)	8–12	-24 individual family sessions, 8 group sessions -Psychoeducation with CBT-based skills building -Promotes enhanced support for child and greater access to service
Adolescents		
Intervention	*Ages*	*Format and goals*
Cognitive Behavior Therapy for Adolescents (CBT-A)* (Feeny et al. 2006)	10–17	-12 sessions -Youth, brief family portion -CBT with psychoeducation, optional focus modules
Dialectical Behavior Therapy for Adolescent (DBT-A)** (Goldstein et al. 2007*; Goldstein et al. 2015**)	14–18	-36 sessions -Mindfulness, distress tolerance, interpersonal effectiveness, problem solving -Youth, family
Family-focused Treatment for Adolescents (FFT-A)** (Miklowitz et al. 2008; Miklowitz et al. 2014)	12–17	-21 sessions -Psychoeducation, family communication, problem solving, reduction of stress, and negative life events
Interpersonal and Social Rhythm Therapy for Adolescents (IPSRT-A)* (Hlastala et al. 2010)	12–18	-16–18 sessions -Minimize effects of life stressors by regular patterns of sleep, exercise, and social interaction -Youth, brief family portion
High-risk Youth		
Intervention	*Ages*	*Format and goals*
FFT-High Risk (FFT-HR)** (Miklowitz et al. 2013)	9–17	-12 sessions -Early identification and intervention for mood symptoms, family communication, problem-solving skills
IPSRT-HR* (Goldstein et al. 2014)	12–18	-Trial study, 12 sessions

Source: Adapted from Division 53, APA; Frías, Palma, and Farriols (2015); Fristad and Macpherson (2014); West and Weinstein (2012); West et al. (2014).
** Indicates randomized control trial (RCT); * Indicates empirically-based, open trial.

Cognitive and Behavioral Interventions

Cognitive Behavioral Therapy for Bipolar Disorder (CBT-BD)

A growing body of research indicates that CBT-BD, when included with pharmacotherapy, is effective in decreasing symptoms and increasing psychosocial functioning (Fristad and MacPherson 2014). CBT-BD models provide youth with multiple skills needed to navigate symptom management and associated difficulties with social, academic, and family functioning. Treatment components include:

1. Psychoeducation for both the patient and the family
2. Affect regulation strategies including mood self-monitoring, recognizing and labeling emotions, and the development of skills for emotional self-regulation
3. Cognitive restructuring techniques including reframing, negative thought-stopping, and positive self-talk
4. Behavioral management strategies
5. Problem-solving skills training
6. Social skills training

Child and Family Focused Cognitive Behavior Therapy (CFF-CBT; West et al. 2009) is a treatment framework specifically designed for 7 to 13-year olds, with bipolar spectrum disorders. It combines individual and parent-focused interventions, with an emphasis on empathic validation. This developmentally sensitive protocol integrates CBT with psychoeducation, interpersonal psychotherapy, mindfulness, and positive psychology techniques. The standard protocol includes 12, 60-minute sessions that address the youth's psychosocial context, and it has been effectively delivered in both individual family (West and Weinstein 2012) and multifamily formats (West et al. 2009). Outcome studies have found increased global functioning and significant reductions in inattentiveness, aggression, mania, psychosis, depression, and sleep disturbance (West et al. 2014).

The acronym RAINBOW conceptualizes key components of CFF-CBT:

Routine: Establishing predictable and simplified routines

Affect Regulation: Psychoeducation about affective circuitry dysfunction, mood monitoring and coping skills to manage mood triggers, and PBSD-specific behavioral-management

I can do it: Enhance child and family self-esteem and self-efficacy

No negative thoughts and live in the now: Use cognitive restructuring and mindfulness to decrease negative or distorted cognitions

Be a good friend or balanced lifestyle for parents: Promote child's social skills and enhance parental balance and self-care

Oh, how can we solve this problem?

Ways to get support: Access support in family, school, and community

Interpersonal and Social Rhythm Therapy (IPSRT)

IPSRT, originally developed by Frank et al. (2005), has been adapted for adolescents with BD (Hlastala and Kotler 2007; Hlastala et al. 2010). IPSRT addresses psychosocial stressors that precipitate or exacerbate mood episodes by disrupting social and sleep routines, and also adapts techniques from interpersonal psychotherapy for depression. Treatment is designed to remediate interpersonal skills deficits and manage mood symptoms to reduce their negative impact on psychosocial functioning. Results from an open study of youth with PBSD, consisting of 16 to 18 sessions over 20 weeks, indicated significant improvements in manic, depressive, and general psychiatric symptoms and improved overall functioning (Hlastala et al. 2010).

Goldstein et al. (2014) applied IPSRT-A to adolescents at high risk for BD due to positive family history in a first-degree relative. Preliminary data indicate that this 12-session intervention contributed to stabilizing daily rhythms and interpersonal relationships for these high-risk youth. The modification of the IPSRT-A manual to this high-risk group is an example of effective, clinically driven adaptations that can be made with EBT.

Other Treatments for Enhancing Emotional Regulation

Dialectical Behavior Therapy (DBT)

Originally developed for adults, DBT (Linehan 1993) may be especially relevant for youth with PBSD due to its core emphasis on addressing emotional intensity, reactivity, and dysregulation. DBT has been adapted for adolescents with bipolar disorders by incorporating illness-specific modifications, differential application of skills based on current mood states, and delivering skills training within a family context (Goldstein et al. 2007). The adolescent protocol consists of 6 months of weekly 60-minute psychotherapy sessions, followed by an additional 6 months of bimonthly sessions to solidify gains. Treatment components of this skills-based approach focus on enhancing skills for:

1. Mindfulness
2. Distress tolerance
3. Emotion regulation
4. Interpersonal effectiveness

A 1-year randomized trial for adolescents with BD indicated that in comparison to counterparts in "psychosocial treatment as usual," youth who participated in DBT showed less severe depressive symptoms and significant decreases in suicidal ideation and nonsuicidal self-injury (Goldstein et al. 2015). Additionally, DBT was associated with enhanced emotional regulation over time and with higher rates of therapy attendance.

Although a comprehensive DBT model entails integration with a team, treatment components may be utilized by an individual practitioner. Other useful resources which address emotional regulation skills, although not specifically designed for PBSD include:

1. *Emotion Regulation in Children and Adolescents* (2013) by Michael Southam-Gerow, PhD.
2. *DBT® Skills Manual for Adolescents* (2015) by Jill Rathus, PhD. and Alec Miller, PsyD., both available at www.guilford.com.

Mood Charting

Charts for monitoring sleep and mood patterns may be incorporated into multiple treatment approaches. A developmentally friendly example is the Mood and Energy Thermometer (Diler 2013), which can be accessed at www.pediatricbipolar.pitt.edu. This thermometer uses ratings on a 1 to 10 scale of both: (1) mania and increased energy, and (2) depression and tiredness, to reflect DSM-5 specification of energy level as a defining criteria of BD. Other sample mood charts, designed to monitor mood, sleep, and medication compliance, are available through bpchildren.com/Charting.html. Free apps for interactive tracking can be found at the following links:

Mood Panda (www.moodpanda.com)
Emoods (www.emoodtracker.com)
Moodlytics (www.moodlytics.com)
Moodtrack (www.emoodtrack.com) (example in Chapter 5, Case Study 4)

Interventions for Neurocognitive Deficits

Pharmacotherapy may address specific neurocognitive deficits as well as mood instability in youth with PBSD. Improvements in sustained attention and cognitive flexibility have been found for adolescents treated with aripiprazole for 24 weeks (Wang et al. 2012). Youth ages 8 to 18 years treated with lamotrigine for 14 weeks showed gains in both working memory and verbal memory, although deficits in attention and executive functions persisted (Pavuluri et al. 2010). Lera-Miguel et al. (2015) found that both processing speed and visual-motor skills in a group of youth with early-onset BD normalized during a 2-year pharmacotherapy period, whereas executive functioning, working memory, and verbal and visual memory remained impaired, relative to typically developing controls (TDCs). Across studies, there is some evidence that atypical antipsychotics may interfere with cognitive performance, whereas anticonvulsants and mood stabilizers may contribute to neurocognitive improvements (Lera-Miguel et al. 2015).

Cognitive remediation, a novel brain-based treatment approach, has been found to improve cognitive functions in adults with BD and children with anxiety and ADHD, although there are, to date, no studies on its generalizability to PBSD (Dickstein et al. 2015). This intervention's emphasis on restructuring neurological networks may have applications for remediating processing deficits common to PBSD.

Interventions for Youth at High-Risk for PBSD

Early identification and treatment implementation for high-risk youth may be particularly effective in moderating the complex and debilitating course of PBSD. Both psychosocial and psychopharmacological interventions have been implemented with youth at high-risk for developing PBSD, due to family risk factors and clinical symptom patterns (Benarous et al. 2016a). One approach to early identification is the clinical staging model used by Bechdolf et al. (2014) to identify adolescents and young adults at "ultrahigh-risk" for BD based on either: (1) subthreshold manic symptoms, (2) depression plus cyclothymic features, or (3) depression plus genetic BD risk. Psychotherapeutic approaches are indicated as the "first line of defense" for these children and adolescents, due to the potential side effects associated with medication regimens.

Intensive Treatment Services—Hospitalization, Residential Placement, and Day Treatment

A clear treatment objective is to maintain the child and adolescent within their home environment, whenever possible, both to maximize stability and to minimize disruptions in routine, as these changes can further exacerbate emotional and behavioral dysregulation. However, psychiatric hospitalization may be needed across illness course for more than 50 percent of children and adolescents with PBSD, driven both by illness severity and limitations in the availability of family and community resources (Shapiro et al. 2014; Vande Voort et al. 2016). The most common clinical presentation leading to hospitalization for youth with bipolar spectrum disorders is mania, particularly psychotic mania, followed by suicidality, and youth with BD-I are particularly likely to require inpatient services (Hirneth et al. 2015; Shapiro et al. 2014).

More intensive levels of care are indicated by:

1. Risk containment for issues of safety and lethality, including:
   a. Severe self-harm and suicidality
   b. Threats or physical violence toward others
2. Severely agitated states and destructive behavior
3. Psychotic symptoms
4. Medication readjustment
5. Limitations in the family environment's capacity for implementing therapeutic services during acute crises

Partial hospitalization or day-treatment programs may also be options for youth who are not a risk to self or others, but are still sufficiently impaired to require intensive treatment.

Finally, residential placements for extended treatment may be utilized when the child or adolescent is not responding adequately to multifaceted outpatient treatment. A list of licensed therapeutic schools and intensive programs is available at www.natsap.org.

Educational Interventions

A majority of youth with PBSD will require special education services, both for emotional and behavioral problems, and for academic difficulties (Wozniak et al. 2013). Within the United States, schools may qualify children and adolescents with PBSD for specialized services under the Individuals with Disabilities Education Act (IDEA) and Section 504 of the Rehabilitation Act of 1973. Youth with PBSD are often designated as "Other Health Impairment (OHI)" or "Emotionally Disturbed (ED)," which does not correspond specifically with a diagnostic category, but rather reflects the child's emotional and behavioral dysregulation. Collaborative consultation within the educational system enhances coordination of multisystemic interventions.

Educational modifications may be made in light of recent neuropsychological findings indicating deficits in cognitive flexibility, sustained attention and information processing found across pediatric bipolar spectrum presentations (Dickstein et al. 2015). Educational resources are provided through bpchildren.com, under the Teachers link, including a download of *The Student With Bipolar Disorder: An Educator's Guide*, with a list of possible accommodations tailored to symptom presentation. Also available through this site is a link to *SWIVEL to Success— Bipolar Disorder in the Classroom: A Teacher's Guide to Helping Students Succeed* (Anglada 2009). The Juvenile Bipolar Research Foundation also provides a link to educational accommodations on the family section of their website, www.jbrf.org. The recently released book *School-Centered Interventions* (Simon 2016) contains a chapter specifically on evidence-based education modifications for youth with PBSD, which may be incorporated into a comprehensive treatment plan.

Supplementary Interventions

Enhancement of the overall physical health of children and adolescents with PBSD has clear implications for improving holistic functioning. Recent findings suggest the potential of aerobic exercise as adjunctive therapy for adolescents with bipolar spectrum disorders, as it was found to positively impact both neural deactivation deficits in attention and activation deficits in inhibition (Metcalfe et al. 2016). This may be particularly beneficial because youth with PBSD are at high risk for developing weight problems and obesity. Therefore, the inclusion of exercise should be encouraged as part of a comprehensive treatment plan. Additionally, the potential mood benefits and tolerability of a multinutrient supplement for PBSD have been indicated in a small open prospective study (Frazier et al. 2013).

Cultural Considerations

Competent treatment of PBSD entails a complex assessment of diversity factors that impact the therapeutic process, including access to services and cultural perspectives of mental health issues, as discussed in Chapter 2. Within a nationally representative U.S. sample, there were no sociocultural differences in treatment utilization for depression or hypo/mania, although non-Hispanic Black youth received less treatment for comorbid psychological problems than did non-Hispanic White youth (Khazanov et al. 2015). This suggests the importance of diversity informed intervention that addresses the full range of symptom presentation of children and adolescents within the bipolar spectrum.

Considerations in Implementing Evidence-Based Treatments

While we strongly encourage practitioners to utilize EBTs when possible, it is important to highlight the difference between treatment *efficacy* and *effectiveness*. *Efficacy* is established by empirically supported evaluations of therapeutic protocols, primarily through well-controlled studies within university and medical centers. *Effectiveness* is shown through implementation research which evaluates the feasibility, acceptability, and generalizability of EBTs to typical clinical settings. The effectiveness of EBTs in community practice is dependent on cost- and time-constraints, compatibility with population needs, and availability of professional resources. As such, adaptability and "flexibility within fidelity" may be used to guide EBT implementation (MacPherson, Leffler, and Fristad 2014).

An additional challenge to the psychologist is that youth treated in community settings tend to have higher comorbidity, greater environmental risks, and more culturally diverse backgrounds than those participating in efficacy studies (Ehrenreich-May and Chu 2014). As such, clinicians working with children and adolescents with PBSD will often need to tailor intervention strategies to address both common psychiatric comorbidities and changes in symptom presentation over time. A careful analysis of barriers to treatment and available resources may help the practitioner tailor interventions which are most likely to be well-received and implemented by the youth and their families.

There is emerging interest in tailoring EBT protocols to meet the specialized needs of both the child and the service delivery system, through implementation of conceptually unified treatments and modular EBT protocols (Bearman and Weisz 2015). Modular approaches may be particularly effective for youth with comorbid presentations, as individual components of empirically validated protocols are selected to optimally fit the youth's changing clinical needs across the course of treatment. Finally, a recent emphasis has been on transdiagnostic treatment, in which common treatment strategies focused on emotional and behavioral regulation, interpersonal efficacy, and effective coping skills are implemented (Ehrenreich-May and Chu 2014). These flexible treatment approaches are also congruent with the Research Domain Criteria (RDoC) reflecting current clinical conceptualization (Garvey, Avenevoli, and Anderson 2016).

Practitioner Summary

1. A multimodal approach which incorporates both psychosocial interventions and pharmacotherapy will maximize treatment outcome, with interprofessional communication to ensure optimal ongoing care.

2. Core components of effective psychotherapy include: (a) symptom reduction, (b) psychoeducation about PBSD, (c) skills-building for emotional and behavioral regulation, (d) positive family communication skills, and (e) reinforcement of ongoing treatment adherence.

3. Intervention approaches should be tailored through the lens of the youth's developmental trajectory, to accommodate changes in verbal proficiency and cognitive complexity.

4. Pharmacotherapy options should be considered in collaboration with the youth's physician, as appropriate medications may directly impact clinical symptoms, while also providing enough stabilization to allow children and adolescents to participate fully in psychosocial interventions.

5. Early treatment is pivotal, including primary intervention of "high-risk" youth and focused secondary intervention in early stages after PBSD diagnosis.

6. Optimal treatment goals are adapted according to illness stage:
   a. Acute, recovery, and maintenance phases
   b. Presentation of hypo/manic versus mixed or depressive symptoms
   c. Level of functional adaptability

7. The psychologist should strive for competency about diversity variables that may differentially impact treatment response.

CHAPTER 5

Case Studies

Case Study 1—Monica

Diagnoses: Bipolar II Disorder

Specific Learning Disorder with Impairment in Mathematics

This case describes a psychoeducational evaluation of a child presenting with a clinical profile of: (1) pediatric bipolar spectrum disorder, (2) average cognitive functioning, and (3) normative academic functioning, with the exception of a mathematical impairment.

Monica is a 7-year-old first grader at a local elementary school. She was referred for assessment due to struggles with emotional dysregulation and impulse control, which created pervasive difficulties throughout all domains of her life. This was observed as unpredictable social behaviors, misinterpretation of social cues and gestures, along with expressions of anger stemming from her affective arousal. When feeling misunderstood, embarrassed, or frustrated these behaviors were exacerbated, only further disrupting her social interactions. Within the classroom Monica is described as having oppositional behaviors including hitting, shoving, flicking, grabbing, kicking, throwing objects, and noncompliance with instructions or requests. These behaviors have been directed toward teachers and staff, as well as students, thus compromising the safety of others. This noncompliance and disrespectful behavior extends beyond the classroom and has been noted on the school bus, both before and after school, and within the home environment. Additional concerns included self-harm, both through verbal statements, "I want to die," and physical behaviors, such as banging her head against walls.

Prior to the psychologist's contact with Monica, a variety of assessments had been conducted through the school district, each focusing on a different behavioral domain: inattention and impulsivity, speech and language, opposition, and developmental social problems. Although some useful data was provided by these behavioral assessments, the complexity of Monica's dysregulation could not be captured by any of these separate categories.

When viewed holistically the emergence of a mood disorder, specifically bipolar spectrum disorder, became apparent. A comprehensive battery was assembled by the psychologist to assess this probable diagnosis, while also determining any cognitive or academic struggles. The battery included: Wechsler Abbreviated Scale of Intelligence–2nd Edition (WASI-II; Wechsler 2011), Wide Range Test of Achievement–4th Edition (WRAT-4; Wilkinson and Robertson 2006), the Child Bipolar Questionnaire (CBQ–Parent report; Papolos et al. 2006), the Jeannie and Jeffrey Illustrated Interview for Children (Papolos, undated), and the Behavioral Assessment System for Children, 3rd Edition (BASC-3—Teacher, Parent and Self reports; Reynolds and Kamphaus 2015).

Assessment results indicated average intellectual abilities for both her verbal and perceptual reasoning skills. Monica's academic performance was also within the average range across domains, with the exception of mathematics, which was found to be an area of weakness; thus she met district-wide criteria for a specific learning disorder in mathematics. Additionally, psychosocial results highlighted her tendency to experience dysregulation of aggressive impulses, deficits in social-emotional problem solving pediatric bipolar features including abrupt and rapid mood swings with emotional outbursts, and clinically significant internalizing behaviors, including the endorsement of suicidality.

In compilation of all testing results, historical data from parents and a school chart review, along with interview data from Monica herself, it was decided that Monica met criteria for pediatric bipolar spectrum disorder, consistent with a diagnosis of BD-II. Monica was transferred to a specialized classroom equipped for such emotional dysregulation and behavioral outbursts. This was a successful transition that enhanced her academic abilities and assisted her in regulating her emotional expression.

Due to her response to multifaceted intervention, including educational accommodations, psychotherapy, and mood-stabilizing medication prescribed by her physician, she was subsequently able to return successfully to a general classroom setting.

Case Study 2—Rafael

Diagnoses: Other Specified Bipolar and Related Disorder

Post-traumatic Stress Disorder

This case study presents a template for effective assessment and intervention with a middle-school boy with Pediatric Bipolar Spectrum Disorder (PBSD) and a complex trauma history. Rafael's debilitating mood symptoms illustrate a clinical profile for which the diagnostic category of "Other Specified Bipolar and Related Disorder" is applicable, as his pattern of mixed symptoms and rapid cycling does not meet criteria for BD-I or BD-II.

Rafael is an 11-year-old boy in the 6th grade, whose guardians initiated an evaluation due to their concerns about his "risk-taking" and "noncompliant" behaviors. The family was not able to provide a clear date when troubling symptoms emerged, but rather noted that the intensity and pervasiveness of his problems had increased steadily over time. Initially, guardians felt that these were likely due to past complex trauma as described below, and provided a therapeutic home milieu, with "love and limits," but sought professional help as problems persisted.

Rafael's legal guardians are his biological paternal aunt and uncle. They obtained guardianship when he was 3 years old, as his biological parents had a history with Child Protective Services due to substance abuse and "child neglect." If a family member was not found to assume parenting responsibilities, Rafael would have been placed in foster care. His aunt and uncle were clearly warmly committed to Rafael, and he calls them "Moms and Pops" to distinguish from his biological parents, "Mama" and "Dad," with whom he has very intermittent and supervised contact.

Both biological parents had dual diagnoses of bipolar disorder and substance abuse. Although it is not certain whether Rafael was exposed to substances in utero, the biological mother drank heavily and used both marijuana and meth during his infancy and preschool years. Rafael was born at 36 weeks' gestation, weighing 6½ pounds. During the first 3 years of his life, his biological parents had a highly conflictual relationship and separated periodically; they fought often and loudly, and law enforcement authorities visited the home multiple times before removing the child. "Moms" and "Pops" were very concerned about the situation, and during that period of time, tried to visit often and have Rafael over for weekends, although they lived several hours away. While Rafael's memories of these early years are partial, he remembers two different times when "Mama" cut her wrists and threatened to drink her blood, before "Dad" was able to call the aunt to come get Rafael. When "Moms" arrived on these two occasions, she found him screaming and hiding behind the couch. Although there is no indication that he was systematically physically abused, he was "spanked" frequently, and often left alone in front of the TV.

Biological father: The biological father has a history of bipolar disorder, with severe depressive episodes and intermittent anger episodes. His mood issues emerged in young adolescence, and he began using alcohol, cannabis and meth regularly by the age of 15. He currently is prescribed Abilify and Prozac, and although he still uses cannabis, is in recovery for alcohol and meth. He completed some college and is trying to restructure his life.

The extended family history of the biological father includes: (1) "Moms" (biological father's sister and Rafael's guardian): Low level depressive symptoms, well managed by psychotherapy and medication, (2) father's older brother: Low level depressive symptoms and diagnosed with attention-deficit/hyperactivity disorder (ADHD), (3) father's youngest sister: Bipolar I disorder, intermittently medicated, (4) father's youngest brother: Severe depressive disorder (question bipolarity), who died in early adulthood due to an accidental overdose.

Biological mother: The mother has a history of bipolar disorder, with severe depression, and was physically abused by her own father. She began using cannabis at age 11 years and added other substances during her high school years. She was previously diagnosed with a learning disability and repeated a grade in school, although she was able to graduate from high school. Extended family psychiatric history of the biological mother is unknown, and she spent substantial periods of her teen years in foster care or group homes.

At the time of intake, Rafael acknowledged headaches, problems getting to sleep and staying asleep, difficulty focusing, hypervigilance, and aggressive episodes, after which he felt extreme remorse. He described racing thoughts, stating "I can't get my mind to shut-off." He also stated that he felt "sad and angry to my Mama," whom he has not seen for more than 2 years, and at times he avoided discussing early distressing memories. He also acknowledged feeling unhappy, fearful, irritated, and nervous, and had periodic nightmares, which were very vivid and often "gory," including zombies and apocalyptic themes.

Assessment was conducted using the Wechsler Intelligence Scale for Children–5th Edition (WISC-V; Wechsler 2014), the Wechsler Individual Achievement Test–3rd Edition (WIAT-III; Wechsler 2009), and the Behavioral Assessment System for Children, 3rd Edition (BASC-3; Reynolds and Kamphaus 2015). Rafael's full scale IQ was in the high average range; he performed slightly below average on the picture span subtest, within the working memory domain, but overall he is clearly a smart young man with many intellectual strengths. His WIAT-III scores were also above average, congruent with his IQ, and his only "average level" was for math fluency, while his oral language was superior.

On the BASC-3, his aunt rated him in the "*clinical*" range on content scales for both emotional self-control and executive functioning. Overall his behavioral symptom index (BSI) was in the "*clinical*" range, with elevations on externalizing and internalizing problems including, attention, hyperactivity, aggression, anxiety, and depression. Congruent with research, his teacher's report was less elevated, although she did note "*at-risk*" symptoms of depression and anxiety and viewed him in the "*at-risk*" range for adaptability including anger control, emotional self-control, and resiliency.

Upon accurate clinical diagnosis, comprehensive intervention was implemented, including: (1) psychoeducation for the family unit, (2) Child-and Family-Focused Cognitive Behavioral Therapy (CFF-CBT), utilizing the RAINBOW techniques described in Chapter 4, and (3) coordination of pharmacotherapy with a child psychiatrist. Additionally, historical trauma issues were processed, with an emphasis on creating a sense of security and mastery.

Case Study 3—Jeanette

Diagnosis: Bipolar II Disorder

This case study describes an adolescent girl who, over the past year, has experienced a notable increase in academic struggles and executive functioning impairment concurrent with an onset of emotional dysregulation. The assessment battery was designed to evaluate cognitive, academic, and executive functioning levels as well as to determine clinical diagnosis in order to guide comprehensive intervention strategies. This presentation highlights the overlap in symptoms of BD and ADHD, and the importance of utilizing a range of assessment instruments to accurately differentiate these disorders.

Jeanette is a 14-year-old girl, beginning her ninth grade year at a local high school. Academics "have never been easy," but her ongoing and central area of concern involves executive functioning deficits including: (1) keeping her assignments organized, (2) planning and prioritizing homework, and (3) being able to successfully complete a project from beginning to end. During middle school she began noticing an exacerbation of these struggles, along with increased difficulty in understanding and completing the academic material that was presented to her. At first she attributed this to the natural progression through the grades, with the accompanying increased case load and expectations. However, she also felt her academic knowledge base was slipping away, and her once successful compensatory skills were weakening. This was causing Jeannette great distress as she transitioned into high school. She began feeling overwhelmed, and her experienced emotions felt intensified. At times she felt like a complete failure and would tell her parents, "I'm too stupid to graduate high school, I'm a huge disappointment to everyone." She experienced these depressed emotional states for approximately two weeks at a time and they typically included self-harm either through risky behaviors or cutting. These periods were followed by a state of "feeling normal, like my normal self." However, the euthymia would then turn into a significant increase in energy and decreased need for sleep. During these periods she wanted to drop out of high school and become a stripper as she would say, "I'm too stupid for school, but dang, I'm sexy. I can make money with this body, who needs school anyway."

Her parents grew very concerned with Jeanette's emotional dysregulation and deterioration of functioning. After speaking with the school psychologist, it was decided that a psychological evaluation could provide insight into Jeannette's functioning. The testing process took longer to complete then what is typical for a 14-year-old. While Jeannette was compliant throughout, her responses often went off topic, which required continual redirection to the task at hand. Once assessment was completed the psychologist provided a feedback session for Jeannette and her parents, and consultation with school staff.

Testing instruments included the Woodcock-Johnson Tests of Achievement IV (WJ-IV-ACH; Schrank et al. 2014), Woodcock-Johnson Tests of Cognitive Abilities IV (WJ-IV-COG; Schrank et al. 2014), Behavior Rating Inventory of Executive Functioning-Second Edition (BRIEF-2; Gioia et al. 2015), and the Child Bipolar Questionnaire (CBQ—Parent report; Papolos et al. 2006). Results revealed that Jeannette's overall IQ fell within the low average range. Impairments were found within language comprehension, auditory processing, and visual-spatial reasoning. In contrast, she revealed strengths in her ability to reason, form concepts, and solve problems that involved unfamiliar or novel information. Academically she had deficits across all domains: reading, writing, and math. Results from the BRIEF-2 showed that Jeannette, her parents, and a teacher consistently endorsed executive functioning deficits across domains. This included her ability to shift, inhibit, exert emotional control, and initiate tasks. Additional impairments were found in her working memory and ability to plan and organize materials. The Child Bipolar Questionnaire, which was only completed by her parents, indicated pediatric bipolar features. This was suggested through their endorsement of Jeannette's rapid and abrupt mood swings, including hypo/mania, depression, poor frustration tolerance, and poor regulation of aggressive impulses. Threats of suicide were also noted and were found to be associated with parent-reports of reckless behavior.

These results were examined in collaboration with Jeannette's current changes in functioning in order to develop a comprehensive treatment plan. This included ongoing participation in Family-focused Treatment for Adolescents (FFT-A), a medication regimen of Saphris as prescribed by her physician, and educational accommodations to provide support for executive functioning deficits.

Case Study 4—Tyrone

Diagnosis: Cyclothymia

This case describes cyclothymia in an adolescent, illustrating the often overlooked symptom presentation of this bipolar spectrum disorder.

Tyrone is a 17-year-old high-school boy who began seeing a psychtherapist due to the stresses generated by the divorce of his parents. The strong therapeutic alliance which was formed allowed Tyrone to feel comfortable and share openly about himself. Throughout this time his therapist noticed a slight inconsistency of his moods. For instance, during some sessions he was more talkative and jovial and during other sessions he was more withdrawn and sullen than usual. Noticing these subtle changes, his therapist asked clarifying questions, such as, "You appear to be in good spirits Tyrone, what made today such a great day?" or "It doesn't seem like you have much energy today Tyrone, I wonder if everything is going ok?" Each time Tyrone was able to acknowledge a shift in his mood, but he was not able to provide additional insight, "Well, some days I have good days, and some days I have bad days." However, he was able to recognize that these "good and bad days" predated his parents' divorce by several years.

Tyrone was given the homework assignment of tracking his "good and bad days" in order to determine any patterns and notable distinct features. After 2 months of mood tracking it was found that every couple of weeks he would experience several days where he felt an increase in energy. He stated, "I didn't think much of it, I just felt like I was rested and ready to take on the world!" During this time he reported feeling "great," he was able to finish his homework in school. He completed his chores at home without being asked, and he stated with a smirk, "I feel pretty confident in myself, I flirt with the girls and tell them what an amazing catch I am."

After these days of feeling accomplished, Tyron found that his mood did indeed change, leaving him feeling tired. He described this by saying, "I dunno, I guess I felt like I had energy and got a lot done, then I was tired, you know, as a consequence of working hard." He reported that he also felt tired for approximately a week and during this time he just wanted to stay in his bed and watch movies. Despite this, he still went to school, but he did not finish his homework in school, in fact, he did not finish his homework at all. He stated, "I think about my parents' divorce a lot during these times, I miss those days when we were all together. But, you know, after awhile I snap out of it." Following this more depressed period Tyron reported feeling "normal" for approximately 2 weeks at a time. During this time his mood was reportedly stable with his typical sleep pattern. He was able to accomplish his responsibilities, both at home and at school, but not at an accelerated pace.

After the pattern and distinct features were discussed, Tyron's treatment plan was changed to reflect the dysregulation of his emotions.

While the fluctuations were subtle and did not severely impair his daily functioning, he desired balance. Future sessions focused on interventions to help him achieve this goal, incorporating interpersonal and social rhythm techniques. The following is reprinted from a mood tracking app, in which Tyron recorded his daily feelings as part of his ongoing treatment process, allowing him to graph his experienced mood fluctuations, and develop mastery over his own symptom management.

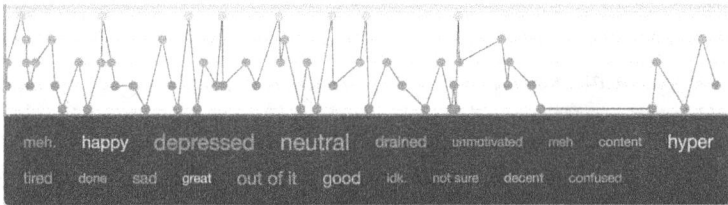

Reprinted from Moodtrack Diary–www.emoodtrack.com

Case Study 5—Rose

Diagnosis: Bipolar I Disorder

This longitudinal case examines the particular challenges of assessment and treatment congruent with the youth's unfolding developmental trajectory. The patient first presented for psychological consultation in kindergarten, and is tracked through her current clinical presentation and adaptive functioning as a high-school student. This comprehensive case addresses multisystemic issues inherent in working with interdisciplinary professionals, and focuses on changes in mood disorder symptomatology through a developmental psychopathology perspective.

Rose was first seen for psychological services at the age of 6 years, as the parents had significant concerns about multiple prodromal symptoms of a pediatric mood disorder, and had heightened awareness due to the bilateral family history of bipolar disorder. Delightfully, Rose came to her first consultation dressed up as a cheetah, complete with tail. While she was often charming, funny, playful and sweet, she switched moods very rapidly, without any apparent external trigger, and erupted in anger easily. Although Rose was very young, a diagnosis of pediatric onset mood disorder was strongly indicated by multiple factors, including:

1. Family's bilateral loading for mood disorder, including three paternal relatives with BD, one maternal relative with BD, and several relatives with depression or ADHD or both.
2. Distinctive prodromal symptom pattern often documented in children who are later diagnosed with PBSD, including: (i) long, intense rages, often lasting up to five hours at a time, (ii) multiple issues with sensory processing, (iii) high emotional reactivity, (iv) early sleep disturbance, (v) high creativity, and (vi) toileting concerns.

Developmental History

Ages 0 to 2 years: Rose was born full-term, with no complications, but showed early signs of sensory oversensitivity and had extreme difficulty establishing a sleep cycle. She also experienced marked separation anxiety, to the extent that she cried up to 6 hours when left by her mother, even when with close family members. She was described as "irritable," "fussy," "a picky eater," and also "charming, cute, and engaged." As a toddler, she had protracted outbursts, tantrums, and rages that would last for 2 to 3 hours several times a week.

Ages 3 to 5 years: As a preschooler, multiple family members and close friends expressed significant concerns, and her grandmother, who had worked in elementary education for many years, commented, "I have never known a child that is this unhappy. Something is seriously wrong." Frequent tantrums, rages and night terrors continued, and mastery of toileting tasks was delayed. She claimed black as her favorite color, and mild hallucinations emerged. Her unmodulated behavior was characterized by restlessness, hyperactivity, and oppositionality, interspersed with periods of remorse and regret for her disruptive actions. She presented as charismatic, verbally precocious, and artistically creative.

Ages 6 to 8½ years: During this time following initial diagnosis and treatment implementation, mood dysregulation progressed, rages increased, and rapid mood cycling became more obvious, with multiple mixed states. Rose experienced frequent thoughts of death and dying, paranoia, pressured talking, creative but tangential wordplay, fascination with morbid themes, and high levels of aggressive behaviors. She began to fall behind academically and had increasingly poor peer relationships. She engaged in periodic destruction of property and ran away several times, once entailing police involvement. Her downward spiral precipitated her first psychiatric placement.

Family Environment

Initially, multiple professionals tended to overemphasize the contributory factors of environmental stress to Rose's symptom presentation. Especially salient is the fact that Rose's older brother, Aaron, has a fairly involved case of cerebral palsy, which has necessitated intensive medical procedures. However, Aaron is an extremely positive influence in Rose's life, and in fact, serves primarily as a protective influence, providing her emotional support and affirmation.

Additionally, this is a warm, intact, and proactive family system which has met the many challenges occasioned by their daughter's psychiatric illness with grace, persistence, and perseverance. They are all very treatment compliant, and have easily and sophisticatedly incorporated treatment recommendations. For example, when introduced to collaborative problem solving (CPS), Rose's parents began using the CPS principles consistently, and in creative ways occasioned by Rose's symptom presentation, and in fact, the mother has even taught and facilitated classes on CPS as a result of her mastery. The lack of professional awareness of reciprocal family transactions and the misinterpretation of "snapshots" during crisis times resulted, unfortunately, in one treatment facility applying a label of "parent-child interaction problem" as a primary diagnostic consideration, which was removed when Rose returned to the care of the ongoing psychologist.

Treatment History

As discussed in the following sections, PBSD was confirmed by ongoing assessments, and intensive psychosocial interventions were implemented. In spite of high motivation and treatment compliance by both Rose and her family, her clinical trajectory has been complex, with only partial symptom remission, even under multifaceted treatment implementation including psychotherapeutic intervention and medication management. The severity of her symptoms has required two psychiatric hospitalizations to date, the first as she was turning 8 years old, due to significant decompensation and disorganization, indicating that a careful adjustment of pharmacotherapy needed to be undergone under close supervision. The second, at the age of 10 years, was necessitated due to suicidal ideation and intent ("I am going to cut my throat with a knife"), and lasted for a week while medication adjustments were made, congruent with decreases in suicidality.

The first hospitalization, which took place as she was turning 8 years, followed a period of marked decline, including aggression toward peers, adults, and her pet, with whom she was typically loving and nurturing. She had a breakdown in the psychologist's office in which she was physically aggressive both to the psychologist and her mother, broke a coffee table, ate soap, play dough and paint, and generally became quite disconnected, angry and confused. She vacillated among emotional states for 2 hours, laughing and giggling uncontrollably, expressing severe rage, and crying and stating she was afraid. On the way to the hospital, she became very elated, talking rapidly and excessively about her "adventure," but during the admission process she cried inconsolably and then began screaming at parents and staff members.

Following a 4-day psychiatric hospitalization, she returned home for 3 months, but as she continued very dysregulated, she was admitted to a residential treatment center with the goal of carefully evaluating and adjusting medications. Residential treatment lasted 2 months. Unfortunately, the medical staff there rejected the ongoing psychologist's and psychiatrist's diagnosis, questioning it due to her age of symptom onset and to her externalizing behavior symptoms. As such, in spite of strong advocacy and interprofessional consultation from her outpatient psychologist and psychiatrist team, the diagnosis within the residential center was changed to one of anxiety disorder, and her mood stabilizer was discontinued, leaving her solely on an SSRI medication. At this point, which was toward the end of her residential stay, her disruptive behaviors had decreased, but she became increasingly more delusional and psychotic, for example seeing eyeballs hanging in her closet and believing that both she and other family members were superheroes with supernatural powers. Fortunately, as soon as she was discharged from treatment, the outpatient team was able to reinstate appropriate medications, and remission of her psychotic symptoms was gradually obtained.

Academic Placement

Rose's educational trajectory has been complex. She initially entered elementary school within a regular classroom, with instructional aides being utilized for support. Her accommodations were initially made under Other Health Impairment as an eligibility status. Following winter break in the second grade, she was transferred to the Behavior Intervention self-contained classroom which was a difficult fit for her, as other special needs peers were primarily within the autism spectrum, and a strict behavioral system was utilized, creating a low possibility of success for her.

For winter semester of the third grade, she received a placement in a specialized day treatment school. She then transitioned to middle school, where she initially had half-day placements in regular classrooms, supplemented by half-days in a contained classroom. She has also attended a day academy specifically designed for students with emotional and behavioral dysregulation issues, where she was very successful. Her academic schedule has been consistently reworked and readjusted, dependent on mood fluctuations. Currently she attends public high school, where she has a combination schedule of specialized socio-emotional learning and mainstream classes.

Psychopharmacology Challenges

To date, Rose has had a trial of 16 different medications, often in combination, in order to address her severe presentation of PBSD. The particular challenges of finding an effective medication regimen were compounded both by the level of her mood dysregulation and by her developmental changes, as multiple medications would provide some level of therapeutic improvement for a time. Table 5.1 indicates pharmacotherapy congruent with her age of intellectual testing. This allows comparison of possible correlations between medication regimens and her cognitive profiles. A partial listing of her past medications includes: Risperidone, Lithobid, Abilify, Celexa, Congentin, Topamax, Geodon, Clonidine, Clonazapam, and Zoloft. Over time, it became clear that antipsychotic medications, while helping with sleep, had a negative side effect profile for her, and ultimately mood stabilizers were more effective and better tolerated. As Rose turned 16 years old, she had a downward trend, with severe and

Table 5.1 Intellectual scores over time as assessed by the WISC-IV

Age	Full scale IQ	Verbal comprehension	Perceptual reasoning	Working memory	Processing speed	Medication status
6	81st percentile	86th percentile	98th percentile	42nd percentile	10th percentile	Unmedicated
7 1/2	73rd percentile	82nd percentile	79th percentile	18th percentile	73rd percentile	Lithium, Abilify, Geodon
8 1/2	86th percentile	90th percentile	70th percentile	16th percentile	58th percentile	Depakote, Catapres
11 3/4	5th percentile	20th percentile	14th percentile	4th percentile	2nd percentile	Depakote, Lamictal, Lexapro, Clonidine, Clonazepam
16	25th percentile	65st percentile	40th percentile	2nd percentile	1st percentile	Lithium, Lamictal, Clonidine

Note: IQ scores are reported as percentiles.

rapid mood shifts and profound struggles coping with daily life. She began engaging in self-injurious behavior, primarily by scratching skin off her arm, and expressed a desire to hurt both herself and others. At this point, her Depakote was increased to stabilize mania, and Lamictal was added. As stabilization was still not obtained, her psychiatrist transitioned her off of Depakote to Lithium, continuing with an addition of Lamictal, including lower doses of Clonidine.

Assessment Results

Cognitive Functioning. Longitudinal neurocognitive results are available, as Rose has received extensive longitudinal services. As seen in the Table 5.1, these provide interesting information about the impact of PBSD and medications on Rose's neurocognitive functioning. Unfortunately, a general theme is a decrease in her cognitive performance on standardized tests and the gradual "slippage" of her academic achievement over time. Although many variables play a contributory role, it is likely that Rose's ability to maintain a steady learning curve has been impacted cumulatively by ongoing severe mood symptoms, medication side effects, and stress generated by developmental lags. Rose's emotional dysregulation, challenges with sustained attention, difficulty with transitions, and periodic emotional and behavioral "melt-downs" have all contributed to difficulty with optimizing cognitive skills and academic achievement.

In sum, Rose's intellectual performance, as assessed by the Wechsler Intelligence Scale for Children–4th Edition (WISC-IV; Wechsler 2013), across multiple time points fluctuated substantially, likely due in part to natural developmental changes, but, most importantly due to the combined impact of her PBSD symptomatology and varying pharmacotherapy regimens. The downward progression of scores generated significant concern for a neuropsychologist, who completed the cognitive testing when Rose was 11¾ years old, and who consequentially proposed a diagnosis of a rare childhood onset dementia, while noting multiple splinter areas of normal functioning. This led to an additional neuro-metabolic evaluation, which ultimately ruled-out a dementia-related illness, and confirmed the ongoing bipolar diagnosis. As seen by the most current results, Rose's cognitive functioning has partially stabilized, although her working memory and processing speed remain low, consistent with research discussed in Chapter 2.

Academic Achievement. Congruent with cognitive testing, multiple time points are available for achievement test results. These are not presented in table format, as different instruments were utilized.

1. Woodcock-Johnson Tests of Achievement-III Battery (Woodcock, Mather, and McGrew 2001) (7½ years, second grade).

   a. Broad Reading   67th percentile
   b. Broad Written Language   42th percentile
   c. Broad Math   22nd percentile

2. Wechsler Individual Achievement Test-III (WIAT-III; Wechsler 2009) (8½ years, third grade).

   a. Overall Achievement   87th percentile
   b. Total Reading   95rd percentile
   c. Written Expression   45th percentile
   d. Mathematics   60th percentile

3. Wide Range Achievement Test-4 (WRAT-4; Wilkinson and Robertson 2006) (11¾ years, fifth grade).

   a. Word Reading   30th percentile
   b. Sentence Comprehension   39th percentile
   c. Math Computation   10th percentile

Behavioral Assessment

1. *ASEBA System* (7 years, 8 months, second grade). Both Rose's teacher and teacher's aide completed the TRF/6-18 (Achenbach and Rescorla 2001). Scores from both respondents indicated that Rose's Total Adaptive Functioning and Academic Performance fell within the "clinically impaired range" (<10th percentile). Further, her symptom profile was in the "clinical range" (>97th percentile) for total problems, internalizing problems, and externalizing problems. Syndrome scales were also in the "clinical range" (>97th percentile) for the following: anxious or depressed, withdrawn or

depressed, social problems, thought problems, attention problems, and aggressive behavior.

Additional quotes from teachers included: "Lovely girl with significant emotional dysfunction and related confusion of thought," and "She wants to be in the spotlight, but shows impulsivity, insecurity, and unpredictability, and as such, has difficulty making and keeping friends."

The CBCL 6/18 (Achenbach and Rescorla 2001) was completed by Rose's mother, with her total competence score falling in the "borderline clinical range" (10th to 16th percentile). Scores for total problems, internalizing, and externalizing problems fell within the "clinical range," as did scales for anxious or depressed, somatic complaints, thought problems, and attention problems. Aggressive behavior was rated in the "borderline clinical range" (93rd to 97th percentile).

2. *ASEBA System* (8½ years, third grade). During the time of her residential placement the Achenbach forms were completed both by her mother (CBCL/6-18) and by her primary residential staff (TRF/6-18) (Achenbach and Rescorla 2001). The mother's CBCL/6-18 indicated significant clinical elevations for: (1) anxious or depressed, (2) attention problems, (3) social problems, and (4) aggressive behavior. Her primary staff also reported clinical scores for: (1) attention problems, (2) social problems, and (3) aggressive behavior.

3. *Behavioral Assessment System for Children—2* (BASC-2; Kamphaus and Reynolds 2007) (11 years, 10 months, fifth grade). Parent ratings for the BASC-2 indicated that all scale scores were in the highly significant clinical range. Adaptive functioning was significantly delayed across all domains, and Rose experienced both auditory and visual hallucinations.

Summary of Checklist Ratings for Behavioral Symptoms. A review of Rose's scores over time on both the ASEBA and the BASC-2 are congruent with research documenting the link between high externalizing scores and PBSD. Further, she presents with the "Juvenile Bipolar

Disorder (JBD)-profile" characterized by clinical elevations on "anxious or depressed," "attention problems," and "aggressive behavior."

Multisystemic Summary

Rose has maintained the same psychologist throughout her treatment, but due to differences in insurance and in treatment setting, has had four different psychiatrists. Her primary psychologist and the family have worked collaboratively to forge positive interprofessional relationships with psychiatrists, pediatricians, and school personnel. Additionally, the family was able to obtain Wrap-A-Round services through the county following discharge from Rose's first psychiatric placement, and these services have been coordinated with the psychologist and with school professionals.

Psychosocial intervention during her elementary and early middle school years was focused on family psychoeducation and CBT-BD. As Rose has transitioned into her teenage years, she has benefited from components of both interpersonal and social rhythm (IPSR) therapy as well as dialectical behavior therapy (DBT) techniques for distress tolerance and emotional regulation. She has an expansive emotional vocabulary, and multiple strategies for self-regulation, but her ability to use these effectively is dependent upon symptom severity.

In closing, throughout her journey through PBSD, Rose has maintained many delightful core qualities. She is funny, affectionate, creative, and loyal. Rose is also motivated to reestablish and repair her important relationships following an emotional or behavioral disruption. Her mother sums her as "a study in contrasts and complexity." Throughout the years of intensive and extensive intervention, through multiple trials of pharmacotherapy, and modifications of her psychotherapy to fit her evolving developmental needs, Rose has developed multiple strategies for living a rich, interesting, and fulfilling life. She has also become a peer advocate for mental health issues. Her transition to young adulthood is likely to be an intricate challenge for Rose and her family, and it is hopeful that her resilience, underlying intelligence, and delightful quirkiness will help make this transition successful. Finally, she was very excited to contribute three pictures which are subsequently presented, which are reflective of her deep sensitivities and artistic nature.

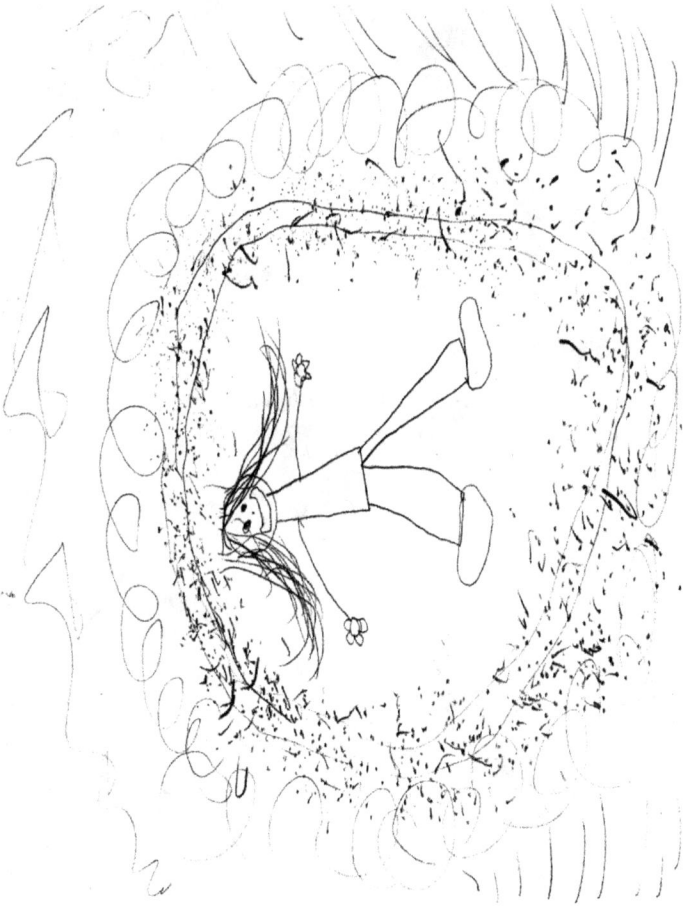

Self-portrait of Rose at age 8 years, in middle of mixed manic episode

Drawing at age 16 years, *"The Lion,"* representative of mixed manic mood state

Drawing at age 16 years, *"The Girl With Wings,"* representative of depressive mood state

Resources

Resources for Clinicians

- *Dialectical Behavior Therapy Skills Training With Adolescents: A Practical Workbook for Therapists, Teens, and Parents* (Eich 2015)
  - A complete skills training manual for DBT with adolescents, focused on practical application for teens, parents, and therapists.
- *FFT-HR: Clinicians' Manual for the Family-Focused Treatment of Children and Adolescents at High Risk for Bipolar Disorder* (Miklowitz, George, and Taylor 2011)
  - This manual presents interventions that have been developed as an evidence-based family approach to treatment of children and youth with bipolar disorders, which is part of a multimodal intervention that typically includes medication.
  - www.semel.ucla.edu/champ/downloads-clinicians
- *Individual-Family Psychoeducational Psychotherapy (IF-PEP): Child Workbook* (Fristad and Goldberg-Arnold 2011)
  - This developmentally-friendly workbook consists of 20 "scripted" 45 to 50-min sessions, and 4 "in-the-bank" sessions.
  - www.moodychildtherapy.com/about-pep/individual-family-groups/
- *Multi-Family Psychoeducational Psychotherapy (MF-PEP): Child Workbook* (Fristad, Goldberg-Arnold, and Leffler 2011)
  - This workbook provides all the integrated materials needed to conduct MF-PEP with children, including teaching materials and child projects.
  - www.moodychildtherapy.com/products/workbooks/
- *Multi-Family Psychoeducational Psychotherapy (MF-PEP): Parent Workbook* (Fristad and Goldberg-Arnold 2011)
  - This workbook includes all the integrated materials needed to conduct MF-PEP with parents, providing teaching

materials, parent, family, and child projects, as well as Coach's Corner, which helps parents coach their children to complete their projects.

o www.moodychildtherapy.com/products/workbooks/

- *Psicoterapia Psicoeducacional Para Familias En Grupo: Libro De Ninos* (Fristad and Goldberg-Arnold 2011)
  o This workbook provides all the integrated materials needed to conduct MF-PEP in Spanish with children, including teaching materials and child projects.
  o www.moodychildtherapy.com/products/workbooks/

- *Psicoterapia Psicoeducacional Para Familias En Grupo: Libro De Trabajo De Los Padres* (Fristad and Goldberg-Arnold 2011)
  o This workbook provides all the integrated materials needed to conduct MF-PEP in Spanish with parents, including teaching materials, parent, family, and child projects, as well as Coach's Corner, which helps parents coach their children to complete their projects.
  o www.moodychildtherapy.com/products/workbooks/

- *Psychotherapy for Children with Bipolar and Depressive Disorders* (Fristad, Goldberg-Arnold, and Leffler 2011)
  o This book provides a wide range of ready-to-use clinical tools for school-age children with bipolar disorder or depression.
  o www.moodychildtherapy.com/products/workbooks/

- *Understanding Bipolar Disorder: A Developmental Psychopathology Perspective* (Miklowitz and Cicchetti 2010)
  o This volume provides up-to-date knowledge about varieties of bipolar disorder and the difficulties and frustrations in diagnosis and treatment.

Websites for Clinicians

- American Academy of Child and Adolescent Psychiatry: http://www.aacap.org/AACAP/Families_and_Youth/ Resource_Centers/Bipolar_Disorder_Resource_Center/ Home.aspx

- Child and Adolescent Bipolar Spectrum Disorders Research and Clinic: www.pediatricbipolar.pitt.edu
- Child and Adolescents Mood Disorders Program: www.semel. ucla.edu/champ/resources
- Psychoeducational Psychotherapy: www.moodychildtherapy. com/professional-resources

Resources for Parents

- *Bipolar Disorder in Children and Teens: A Parent's Guide* (2013). NIMH, U.S. Department of Health & Human Services. Publication No. 08-6380.
- "No Letting Go" (2016)—A movie based on a true story of a boy with PBSD, adapted from the short documentary "Illness."
  - o Available at www.bphope.com/kids-children-teens/movie-no-letting go/

Books for Parents

- *If Your Child is Bipolar: The Parent-to-Parent Guide to Living with and Loving a Bipolar Child* (Singer and Gurrentz 2003)
  - o A practical and supportive guide that empowers parents as they struggle with a child with mood disorder.
- *It's Nobody's Fault* (Koplewicz 2010)
  - o Describes 13 common psychiatric disorders in children, and outlines the diagnostic and treatment process in a no-fault manner.
- *New Hope for Children & Teens with Bipolar Disorder* (Birmaher 2013)
  - o Provides compassionate and informative methods to help manage the diagnosis of PBSD and develop the natural strengths, gifts, and skills that every child has to offer.
- *Raising a Moody Child: How to Cope with Depression and Bipolar Disorder* (Fristad and Goldberg-Arnold 2012)

o Describes the diagnosis, professional treatment, and relevant coping strategies for a mood disordered child and his or her family.

- *Straight Talk About Psychiatric Medications for Kids-Fourth Edition* (Wilen and Hammerness 2016)
  o An educational guide that outlines diagnosis, treatment, and medication strategies for a variety of childhood disorders.
- *The Bipolar Child* (Papolos and Papolos 2007)
  o Provides a compendium of information on bipolar disorder and its treatment in youth.
- *The Bipolar Disorder Survival Guide* (Miklowitz 2010)
  o Provides current information and practical problem-solving advice addressing bipolar symptoms, medications, and the impact within the daily life of home and work.
- *The Bipolar Handbook for Children, Teens, and Families: Real-Life Questions with Up-to-Date Answers* (Burgess 2008)
  o A practical resource for children and teens affected by bipolar disorder.
- *The Bipolar Teen: What You Can Do to Help Your Child and Your Family* (Miklowitz and George 2007)
  o Describes the diagnosis, professional treatment, and relevant coping strategies for adolescents with bipolar disorder and their families. Includes an extensive "Resource" section, with references to relevant educational services, residential treatment facilities, and outpatient treatment.
- *The Childhood Bipolar Disorder Answer Book: Practical Answers to the Top 300 Questions Parents Ask* (Anglada and Hakala 2008)
  o Written in question-and-answer format by the parent of two children with bipolar disorder and a psychiatrist who treats mood disordered children.
- *The Explosive Child. A New Approach for Understanding and Parenting Easily Frustrated, Chronically Inflexible Children* (Greene 2014)
  o Facilitates the understanding of why and when children have challenging behaviors, and how to respond in

ways that are nonpunitive, nonadversarial, humane, and effective.

- *The Ups and Downs of Raising a Bipolar Child: A Survival Guide for Parents* (Lederman and Fink 2007)
  - o Provides caregivers with psychoeducation and advice on how to cope with specialized PBSD issues, while providing guidelines on obtaining care and support for both the child and the family.

Resources for Adolescents

- *Don't Let Your Emotions Run Your Life for Teens: Dialectical Behavior Therapy Skills for Helping You Manage Mood Swings, Control Angry Outbursts and Get Along with Others* (Van Dijk 2011)
  - o Workbook based on dialectical behavior therapy (DBT), providing multiple techniques to help adolescents develop skills for mindfulness, distress tolerance, and emotional regulation.
- *Intense Minds: Through the Eyes of Young People with Bipolar Disorder* (Anglada 2009)
  - o A collection of personal reflections by adolescents and young adults describing the experience of mania and depression.
- *Recovering from Depression: A Workbook for Teens* (Copeland and Copans 2002)
  - o A workbook to help adolescents understand depression and learn coping strategies.
- *The Bipolar Workbook for Teens: DBT Skills to Help You Control Mood Swings* (Van Dijk and Guindon 2010)
  - o Includes exercises and worksheets that teach skills drawn from dialectical behavior therapy (DBT). DBT skills can help teens with bipolar disorder improve their relationships with friends and family and calm themselves when their emotions get really overwhelming.
- *The Storm in My Brain* (Joachim 2003) (dbsalliance.org/pdfs/storm.pdf)

o Downloadable book with art by youth with bipolar spectrum disorders.

Books for Adolescents

- *Mind Race: A Firsthand Account of One Teenager's Experience with Bipolar Disorder* (Jamieson 2006)
  o Autobiography interwoven with facts about bipolar disorder and its treatment.
- *The Phoenix Dance* (Calhoun 2005)
  o Fiction based on the Grimms' Twelve Dancing Princesses, explores the experience of bipolar disorder in an adolescent girl.
- *When Nothing Matters Anymore: A Survival Guide for Depressed Teens* (Cobain 1998)
  o A two-part book that describes depression and its treatment strategies.

Resources for Children

- www.bpchildren.com
  o Resource and support site for families coping with PBSD.
  o Includes multiple audio/video resources
  o Links to youth appropriate books including:
    - *Brandon and the Bipolar Bear (also available in a DVD storytelling format)*
    - *Anger Mountain*
    - *My Roller Coaster Feelings Book and Workbook*
  o Offers mood charts, posters, and a newletter

Books for Children

- *Anger Mountain* (Hebert 2005)
  o A short story to help young children understand and deal with angry feelings.
- *Brandon & the Bipolar Bear* (Anglada 2011)
  o A storybook about a young boy newly diagnosed with bipolar disorder.

- *Don't Let your Emotions Run Your Life for Kids: A DBT-based Skills Workbook to Help Children Manage Mood Swings, Control Angry Outbursts, and Get Along With Others* (Solin and Kress 2017)
  - o Written for children ages 7 to 12 years to use along with their caregivers, this workbook contains 37 hand-on activities to help children develop an emotional skills toolbox for dealing with intense emotions.
- *Matt, The Moody Hermit Crab* (McGee 2002)
  - o A chapter book designed for 8 to 12-year-olds that portrays the depressive and manic phases of bipolar disorder.
- *My Bipolar Roller Coaster Feelings Book & Workbook* (Hebert 2005)
  - o A storybook about a young boy diagnosed with bipolar disorder and accompanying workbook to help children better understand bipolar disorder.
- *The Storm in My Brain* (Joachim 2003) (dbsalliance.org/pdfs/storm.pdf)
  - o Downloadable book with art by youth with bipolar spectrum disorders

Resources for Educators

- *Educating and Nurturing the Bipolar Child* (Papolos, 2001)
  - o DVD available from the Juvenile Bipolar Research Foundation discussing strategies to help youth within the school setting.
- *From Emotions to Advocacy: The Special Education Surviving Guide* (Wright and Wright 2006)
  - o Provides a how-to for seeking appropriate school services for children with special needs.
- *SWIVEL to Success—Bipolar Disorder in the Classroom: A Teacher's Guide to Helping Students Succeed* (Anglada 2009)
  - o Describes the impact of bipolar disorder on a student in the classroom and suggests school-based interventions.

School and Education Resources

- http://www.dbsalliance.org/site/PageServer?pagename=bmpn_learn_family_resources - Depression and Bipolar Support Alliance, includes education topics
- www.iser.com/index.shtml—Internet Special Education Resources (ISER)
- www.natsap.org—National Association of Therapeutic Schools and Programs

Information on Educational Accommodations

- International Bipolar Foundation: http://ibpf.org/article/accommodations-students-bipolar-disorder-and-related-disabilities
- Juvenile Bipolar Research Foundation: www.jbrf.org/page-for-families/educational-issues-facing-children-with-bipolar-disorder/symptoms-and-accomodations/
- The Bipolar Child: http://bipolarchild.com/resources/model-iep/

Additional Websites

- BP Magazine: Hope and Harmony for People with Bipolar: www.bphope.com
  o Includes resource section on bipolar disorder in children and teens.
- BPChildren: www.bpchildren.com Extensive resources and links for children, adolescents, parents, and teachers.
- Brain and Behavior Research Foundation: www.bbrfoundation.org
- Juvenile Bipolar Research Foundation: www.bpchildresearch.org
- National Alliance on Mental Illness: www.nami.org
- National Institute of Mental Health: www.nimh.nih.gov
- The Depression and Bipolar Support Alliance (DBSA): www.dbsalliance.org.

Multiple resources for clinicians, parents, and youth, including:
  o *DBSA Wellness Tracker*
  o *Wellness Toolbox*
  o *Facing Us Clubhouse*
  o *Access to the CMRS, Parent Version*
- UCLA Mood Disorders Research Program: www.semel.ucla. edu/mood/research-program
- UCLA Youth Stress and Mood Program: www.semel.ucla. edu/mood/youth-stress
- www.nami.org. The nation's leading grassroots, self-help, and family advocacy organization dedicated to improving the lives of people with brain disorders. NAMI is active in the research and political arenas and campaigns actively against discrimination and for access to treatment.

Links to Online Parent Support Community

- Bipolar Disorder Resource Center, American Academy of Child & Adolescent Psychiatry: www.aacap.org/AACAP/Families_and_Youth/Resource_ Centers/Bipolar_Disorder_Resource_Center/Home.aspx
- Child and Adolescent Bipolar Foundation: http://bipolarchild.com/resources/online-resources/_
- Depression and Bipolar Support Alliance: www.dbsalliance.org/site/PageServer?pagename=peer_ support_group_locator
  o Balanced Mind Parent Network
  o BMPN hosts 11 online support communities
- The Balanced Mind Parent Network (a program of DBSA): www.thebalancedmind.org/
- National Alliance on Mental Illness: www.nami.org/Find-Support/NAMI-Programs/NAMI-Family-Support-Group
- National Institute of Mental Health (NIMH): www.nimh.nih.gov/health/publications/bipolar-disorder-in-children-and-teens-easy-to-read/index.shtml

References

Achenbach, T.M. 1991a. *Manual for the Child Behavior Checklist/4–18 and 1991 Profile*. Burlington, VT: University of Vermont, Department of Psychiatry.

Achenbach, T.M. 1991b. *Manual for the Youth Self-Report Form and 1991 Profile*. Burlington, VT: University of Vermont, Department of Psychiatry.

Achenbach, T.M. 1991c. *Manual for the Teacher's Report Form and 1991 Profile*. Burlington, VT: University of Vermont, Department of Psychiatry.

Achenbach, T.M. 2009. *The Achenbach System of Empirically Based Assessment (ASEBA): Development, Findings, Theory, and Applications*. Burlington, VT: University of Vermont Research Center for Children, Youth, & Families.

Achenbach, T.M., and L.A. Rescorla. 2001. *Manual for the ASEBA School-Age Forms & Profiles*. Burlington, VT: University of Vermont.

Adleman, N.E., S.J. Fromm, V. Razdan, R. Kayser, D.P. Dickstein, M.A. Brotman, and E. Leibenluft. 2012. "Cross-sectional and Longitudinal Abnormalities in Brain Structure in Children With Severe Mood Dysregulation or Bipolar Disorder." *Journal of Child Psychology & Psychiatry* 53, no. 11, pp. 1149–56. doi:10.1111/j.1469-7610.2012.02568.x

Adleman, N.E., A.K. Kayster, A.K. Olsavsky, B.L. Bones, E.J. Muhrer, S.J. Fromm, and M.A. Brotman. 2013. "Abnormal Fusiform Activation During Emotional-Face Encoding Assessed With Functional Magnetic Resonance Imaging." *Psychiatry Research Journal* 212, pp. 161–63. doi:10.1016/j.pscychresns.2013.01.006

Agnew-Blais, J., and A. Danese. 2016. "Childhood Maltreatment and Unfavourable Clinical Outcomes in Bipolar Disorder: A Systematic Review and Meta-Analysis." *The Lancet Psychiatry* 3, no. 4, pp. 342–49. doi:org/10.1016/S2215-0366(15)00544-1

Algorta, G.P., E.A. Youngstrom, J. Phelps, M.M. Jenkins, J.K. Youngstrom, and R.L. Findling. 2013. "An Inexpensive Family Index of Risk for Mood Issues Improves Identification of Pediatric Bipolar Disorder." *Psychological Assessment* 25, pp. 120–22. doi:10.1037/a00292256-27

Alloy, L.B., R.E. Bender, W.G. Whitehouse, C.A. Wagner, R.T. Liu, D.A. Grant, and L.Y. Abramson. 2012. "High Behavioral Approach System (BAS) Sensitivity, Reward Responsiveness, and Goal-Striving Predict First Onset of Bipolar Spectrum Disorders: A Prospective Behavioral High-Risk Design." *Journal of Abnormal Psychology* 121, pp. 339–51. doi:10.1037/a0025877

Alloy, L.B., E.M. Boland, T.H. Ng, W.G. Whitehouse, and L.Y. Abramson. 2015. "Low Social Rhythm Regularity Predicts First Onset of Bipolar Spectrum

Disorders Among At-Risk Individuals With Reward Hypersensitivity." *Journal of Abnormal Psychology* 124, no. 4. pp. 944–52. doi:10.1037/jabn000010

Alloy, L.B., R. Nusslock, and E.M. Boland. 2015. "The Development and Course of Bipolar Spectrum Disorders: An Integrated Reward and Circadian Rhythm Dysregulation Model." *Annual Review of Clinical Psychology* 11, pp. 213–50. doi:10.1146/annurev-clinpsy-032814-112902

American Academy of Child and Adolescent Psychiatry. 2007. "Practice Parameters for the Assessment and Treatment of Children and Adolescents with Bipolar Disorders." *Journal of the American Academy of Child and Adolescent Psychiatry* 46, no. 1, pp. 107–25.

American Educational Research Association, *American Psychological Association, & National Council on Measurement in Education.* 2014. Standards for Educational and Psychological Testing. Washington, DC: American Educational Research Association.

American Psychiatric Association. 2013. *Diagnostic and Statistical Manual of Mental Disorders.* 5th ed. Washington, DC: Cambridge.

Anand, A., D.L. Koller, W.B. Lawson, E.S. Gershon, and J.I. Nurnberger. 2015. "Genetic and Childhood Trauma Interaction Effect on Age of Onset in Bipolar Disorder: An Exploratory Analysis." *Journal of Affective Disorders* 179, pp. 1–5. doi:10.1016/j.jad.2015.02.029

Anglada, T. 2009. *SWIVEL to Success—Bipolar Disorder in the Classroom: A Teacher's Guide to Helping Students Succeed.* Murdock, FL: BPChildren.

Angold, A., and J.E. Costello. 2000. "The Child and Adolescent Psychiatric Assessment." *Journal of the American Academy of Child & Adolescent Psychiatry* 39, pp. 39–48. doi:10.1097/00004583-200001000-00015

Angold, A., M. Prendergast, M. Rutter, and E. Simonoff. 2008. *Child and Adolescent Psychiatric Assessment (CAPA), Child Interview Version 5.0.* Durham, NC: Developmental Epidemiology Program, Duke University.

Angst, J., R. Adolfsson, F. Benazzi, A. Gamma, E. Hantouche, T.D. Meyer, P. Skeppar, E. Vieta, and J. Scott. 2005. "The HCL-32: Towards a Self-Assessment Tool for Hypomanic Symptoms in Outpatients." *Journal of Affective Disorders* 88, no. 2, pp. 217–33. doi:10.1016/j.jad.2005.05.011

Arango, C., D. Fragues, M. Parellada. 2014. "Differential Neurodevelopmental Trajectories in Patients with Early-Onset Bipolar and Schizophrenia Disorders." *Schizophrenia Bulletin* 40, no. 2, pp. 138–46. doi:10.1093/schbul/sbt198

Axelson, D., B.J. Birmaher, D. Brent, S. Wassick, C. Hoover, J. Bridge, and N. Ryan. 2003. "A Preliminary Study of the Kiddie Schedule for Affective Disorders and Schizophrenia for School-Age Children Mania Rating Scale for Children and Adolescents." *Journal of Child and Adolescent Psychopharmacology* 13, no. 4, pp. 463–70. doi:http://dx.doi.org.georgefox.idm.oclc.org/10.1089/104454603322724850

Axelson, D.A., B. Birmaher, M.A. Strober, B.I. Goldstein, W. Ha, M.K. Gill, and M.B. Keller. 2011. "Course of Subthreshold Disorder in Youth: Diagnostic Progression from Bipolar Disorder not Otherwise Specified." *Journal of the American Academy of Child & Adolescent Psychiatry* 50, no. 10, pp. 1001–16. doi:10.1016/j.jaac.2011.07.005

Axelson, D., B. Birmaher, J. Zelazny, J. Kaufman, and M.K. Gill. 2009. *The Schedule for Affective Disorders and Schizophrenia—Present and Lifetime Version (K-SADS-PL) 2009 Working Draft.* Advanced Center for Intervention and Services Research, Western Psychiatric Institute and Clinic. University of Pittsburgh Department of Psychiatry Website: http://www.wpic.pitt.edu/research/AssessmentTools/ChildAdolescent/ksads_pl_2009.htm

Baldessarini, R.J., L. Tondo, G.H. Vazquez, J. Undurraga, L. Bolzani, A. Yildiz, and T. Mauricio. 2012. "Age at Onset Versus Family History and Clinical Outcomes in 1,665 International Bipolar-I Disorder Patients." *World Psychiatry* 11, pp. 40–46. doi:10.1016/j.wpsyc.2012.01.006

Baroni, A., M. Hernandez, M.C Grant, and G.L. Faedda. 2012. "Sleep Disturbances in Pediatric Bipolar Disorder: A Comparison Between Bipolar I and Bipolar NOS." *Frontiers in Psychiatry* 3, p. 22. doi:10.3389/fpsyt.2012.00022

Bearman, S.K., and J.R. Weisz. 2015. "Review: Comprehensive Treatments for Youth Comorbidity—Evidence-Guided Approaches to a Complicated Problem." *Child & Adolescent Mental Health* 20, no. 3, pp. 131–41. doi:10.1111/camh.12092

Bechdolf, A., A. Ratheesh, S.M. Cotton, B. Nelson, A.M. Chanen, J. Betts, and P.D. McGorry. 2014. "The Predictive Validity of Bipolar at-Risk (Prodromal) Criteria in Help-Seeking Adolescents and Young Adults: A Prospective Study." *Bipolar Disorder* 16, pp. 493–504. doi:10.1111/bdi.12205

Belardinelli, C., J.P. Hatch, R.L. Olvera, M. Fonseca, S.C. Caetano, M. Nicoletti, and J.C. Soares. 2008. "Family Environment Patterns in Families with Bipolar Children." *Journal of Affective Disorders* 107, pp. 299–305. doi:10.1016/j.jad.2007.08.011

Benarous, X., A. Consoli, V. Milhiet, and D. Cohen. 2016a. "Early Interventions for Youths at High Risk for Bipolar Disorder: A Developmental Approach." *European Child & Adolescent Psychiatry* 25, no. 3, pp. 217–33. Available from: Psychology and Behavioral Sciences Collection, Ipswich, MA (accessed June 18, 2016).

Benarous, X., N. Mikita, R. Goodman, and A. Stringaris. 2016b. "Distinct Relationships Between Social Aptitude and Dimensions of Manic-Like Symptoms in Youth." *European Journal of Child & Adolescent Psychiatry* 25, no. 8, pp. 831–42. doi:10.1007/s00787-015-0800-7

Bernstein, B.E., and C. Pataki. 2015. "Pediatric Bipolar Affective Disorder Clinical Presentation." *Medscape*. http://emedicine.medscape.com/article/913464-clinical

Bhowmik, D., R.R. Aparasu, S.S. Rajan, J.T. Sherer, M. Ochoa-Perez, and H. Chen. 2014. "Risk of Manic Switch Associated with Antidepressant Therapy in Pediatric Bipolar Depression." *Journal of Child and Adolescent Psychopharmacology* 24, no. 10, pp. 551–61. doi:10.1089/cap2014.0028

Biederman, J., S.V. Faraone, C. Petty, M. Martelon, K.Y. Woodworth, and J. Wozniak. 2013a. "Further Evidence that Pediatric-Onset Bipolar Disorder Comorbid with ADHD Represents a Distinct Subtype: Results from a Large Controlled Family Study." *Journal of Psychiatric Research* 47, no. 1, pp. 15–22. doi:10.1016/j.jpsychires.2012.08.002

Biederman, J., M. Martelon, S.V. Faraone, K.Y. Woodworth, T.J. Spencer, and J.R. Wozniak. 2013b. "Personal and Familial Correlates of Bipolar (BP)-1 Disorder in Children with a Diagnosis of BP-1 Disorder with a Positive Child Behavior Checklist (CBCL)-Severe Dysregulation Profile: A Controlled Study." *Journal of Affective Disorders* 147, nos. 1–3, pp. 164–70. doi:10.1016/j.jad.2012.10.028

Biederman, J., C. Petty, M.C. Monuteaux, M. Evans, T. Parcell, S.V. Faraone, and J. Wozniak. 2009. "The CBCL-Pediatric Bipolar Disorder Profile Predicts a Subsequent Diagnosis of Bipolar Disorder and Associated Impairments in ADHD Youth Growing Up: A Longitudinal Analysis." *Journal of Clinical Psychiatry* 70, pp. 732–40. doi:10.4088/JCP.08m04821

Birleson, P. 1981. "The Validity of Depressive Disorder in Childhood and the Development of a Self-Rating Scale: A Research Report." *Journal of Child Psychology and Psychiatry* 22, no. 1, pp. 73–88. doi:10.1111/j.1469-7610.1981.tb00533.x

Birleson, P., I. Hudson, D.G. Buchanan, and S. Wolff. 1987. "Clinical Evaluation of a Self-Rating Scale for Depressive Disorder in Childhood (Depression Self-Rating Scale)." *Journal of Clinical Psychology & Psychiatry* 28, no. 1, pp. 43–60. doi:10.1111/j.1469.7610.1987.tb00651.x

Birmaher, B. 2013. "Bipolar Disorder in Children and Adolescents." *Child and Adolescent Mental Health* 18, pp. 140–48. doi:10.1111/camh.12021

Birmaher, B., D. Axelson, B. Goldstein, K. Monk, C. Kalas, M. Obreja, and D. Kupfer. 2010. "Psychiatric Disorders in Preschool Offspring of Parents with Bipolar Disorder: The Pittsburgh Bipolar Offspring Study (BIOS)." *American Journal Of Psychiatry* 167, no. 3, pp. 321–30. doi:10.1176/appi.ajp.2009.09070977

Birmaher, B., D. Axelson, B. Goldstein, M. Strober, M.K. Gill, J. Hunt, and M. Keller. 2009. "Four-Year Longitudinal Course of Children and Adolescents with Bipolar Spectrum Disorders: The Course and Outcome of Bipolar Youth (COBY) Study." *The American Journal of Psychiatry* 166, no. 7, pp. 795–804. doi:10.1176/appi.ajp.2009

Birmaher, B., M.K. Gill, D.A. Axelson, B.I. Goldstein, T.R. Goldstein, H. Yu, and M. Keller. 2014. "Longitudinal Trajectories and Associated Baseline Predictors in Youths with Bipolar Spectrum Disorders." *American Journal of Psychiatry* 17, no. 3, pp. 990–99. doi:10.1176/appi.ajp.2014.13121577

Carlson, G.A., and D.N. Klein. 2014. "How to Understand Divergent Views on Bipolar Disorder in Youth." *Annual Review of Clinical Psychology* 10, pp. 529–51. doi:10.1146/annurev-clinpsy-032813-153702

Carlson, G.A., and C. Pataki. 2015. "Presentation of Mania/Bipolar I in Youth: Comparison with Adults." In *Bipolar Disorder in Youth: Presentation, Treatment, & Neurobiology*, eds. S.M. Strakowski, M.P. DelBello, and C.M. Adler, pp. 13–33. New York: Oxford University Press.

Chang, K.D., A. Garrett, and M. Singh. 2014. "Neurobiological Clue of Risk for Bipolar Disorder Development." *Psychiatric Annals* 4, no. 10, pp. 466–70. doi:10.3928/00485713-20141003-05

Cooperberg, M. 2004. *Clinically Significant Change for Outcome Measures Used with Pediatric Bipolar Disorders.* ProQuest Dissertations and Theses.

Correll, C.U., D.M. Olvet, A.M. Auther, M. Hauser, T. Kishimoto, R.E. Carrión, B.A. Cornblatt. 2014. "The Bipolar Prodrome Symptom Interview and Scale–Prospective (BPSS-P): Description and Validation in a Psychiatric Sample and Healthy Controls." *Bipolar Disorder* 16, pp. 505–22. doi:10.1111/bdi.12209

Cox, J.H., S. Seri, and A.E. Cavanna. 2014. "Clinical Guidelines on Long-Term Pharmacotherapy for Bipolar Disorder in Children and Adolescents." *Journal of Clinical Medicine* 3, no. 1, pp. 135–43. doi:10.3390/jcm3010135

Danielson, C.K., E.A. Youngstrom, R.L. Findling, and J.R. Calabrese. 2003. "Discriminative Validity of the General Behavior Inventory Using Youth Report." *Journal of Abnormal Child Psychology* 31, pp. 29–39. doi:10.1023/A:1021717231272

de Dios, C., J.M. Goikolea, F. Colom, C. Moreno, and E. Vieta. 2014. "Bipolar Disorders in the New DSM-5 and ICD-11 Classifications. Los Trastornos Bipolares En Las Nuevas Clasificaciones: DSM-5 y CIE-11." *Revista de Psiquiatría y Salud Mental* 7, no. 4, pp. 179–85.

DeFilippis, M., and K.D. Wagner. 2015. "The Treatment of Preschool Mood Disorders." *Current Treatment Options in Psychiatry* 2, no. 1, pp. 57–72. doi:10.1007/s40501-015-0036-7

Demeter, C.A., E.A. Youngstrom, G.A. Carlson, T.W. Frazier, B.M. Rowles, J. Lingler, and R.L. Findling. 2013. "Age Differences in the Phenomenology of Pediatric Bipolar Disorder." *Journal of Affective Disorders* 147, nos. 1–3, pp. 295–303. doi:10.1016/j.jad.2012.11.021

Depue, R.A., S. Krauss, M.R. Spoont, and P. Arbisi. 1989. "General Behavior Inventory Identification of Unipolar and Bipolar Affective Conditions in a Nonclinical University Population." *Journal of Abnormal Psychology* 98, pp. 117–26. doi:10.1037/0021-843X.98.2.117

Deveney, C.M., M.A. Brotman, A.M. Decker, D.S. Pine, and E. Leibenluft. 2012. "Affective Prosody Labeling in Youths with Bipolar Disorder or Severe Mood Dysregulation." *Journal of Child Psychology and Psychiatry* 53, no. 3, pp. 262–70. doi:10.1111/j.1469-7610.2011.02482.x

Díaz-Caneja, C.M., C. Moreno, C. Llorente, A. Espliego, C. Arango, and D. Moreno. 2014. "Practitioner Review: Long-Term Pharmacological Treatment of Pediatric Bipolar Disorder." *Journal of Child Psychology and Psychiatry* 55, pp. 959–80. doi:10.1111/jcpp.12271

Dickstein, D.P., D. Axelson, A.B. Weissman, S. Yen, J.I. Hunt, B.I. Goldstein, and M.B. Keller. 2016. "Cognitive Flexibility and Performance in Children and Adolescents with Threshold and Sub-Threshold Bipolar Disorder." *European Child and Adolescent Psychiatry* 25, no. 6, pp. 625–38. doi:10.1007/s00787-015-0769-2

Dickstein, D.P., G.K. Cushman, K.L. Kim, A.B. Weissman, and E. Wegbreit. 2015. "Cognitive Remediation: Potential Novel Brain-based Treatment for Bipolar Disorder in Children and Adolescents." *CNS Spectrums* 20, pp. 382–390.

Diler, R.S. 2013. *Mood and Energy Thermometer*. At www.pediatricbipolar.pitt.edu

Diler, R.S., and B. Birmaher. 2012. "Bipolar Disorder in Children and Adolescents." In *IACAPAP e-textbook of Child and Adolescent Mental Health*, ed. J.M. Rey. Geneva: International Association for Child and Adolescent Psychiatry and Allied Professions.

Diler, R.S., B. Birmaher, D. Axelson, B. Goldstein, M. Gill, M. Strober, and M.B. Keller. 2009. "The Child Behavior Checklist (CBCL) and the CBCL-Bipolar Phenotype Are Not Useful in Diagnosing Pediatric Bipolar Disorder." *Journal of Child & Adolescent Psychopharmacology* 19, pp. 23–30. doi:10.1089/cap.2008.067

Diler, R.S., C.D. Ladouceur, A. Segreti, J.R.C. Almeida, B. Birmaher, D.A. Axelson, M.L. Phillips, and L.A. Pan. 2013. "Neural Correlates of Treatment Response in Depressed Bipolar Adolescents During Emotion Processing." *Brain Imaging and Behavior* 7, no. 2, pp. 227–35. doi:10.1007/s11682-012-9219-7

Dorfman, J., and A. Robb. 2016. "Long-Term Treatment Strategies for Pediatric Bipolar Disorder." *Current Treatment Options in Psychiatry* 3, no. 2, pp. 206–20. doi:10.1007/s40501-016-0080-y

Doucette, S., J. Horrocks, P. Grof, C. Keown-Stoneman, and A. Duffy. 2013. "Attachment and Temperament Profiles Among the Offspring of a Parent with Bipolar Disorder." *Journal of Affective Disorders* 150, no. 2, pp. 522–26. doi:10.1016/j.jad.2013.01.023

Ehrenreich-May, J., and B.S. Chu. 2014. *Transdiagnostic Treatments for Children and Adolescents: Principles and Practice*. New York: Guilford Press.

Ellis, B.J., W.T. Boyce, J. Belsky, M.J. Bakermans-Kranenburg, and M.H. Van IJzendoorn. 2011. "Differential Susceptibility to the Environment: An Evolutionary-Neurodevelopmental Theory." *Development and Psychopathology* 23, no. 1, pp. 7–28. doi:10.1017/S0954579410000611

Ellis, A.J., L.C. Portnoff, D.A. Axelson, R.A. Kowatch, P. Walshaw, and D.J. Miklowitz. 2014. "Parental Expressed Emotion and Suicidal Ideation in Adolescents with Bipolar Disorder." *Psychiatry Research* 216 no. 2, pp. 213–16. doi:10.1016/j.psychres.2014.02.013

Esposito-Smythers, C., T. Goldstein, B. Birmaher, B. Goldstein, J. Hunt, N. Ryan, and M. Keller. 2010. "Clinical and Psychosocial Correlates of Non-Suicidal Self-Injury within a Sample of Children and Adolescents with Bipolar Disorder." *Journal of Affective Disorders* 125, nos. 1–3, pp. 89–97. doi:10.1016/j.jad.2009.12.029

Faraone, S.V., R.R. Althoff, J.J. Hudziak, M. Monuteaux, and J. Biederman. 2005. "The CBCL PDSM Bipolar Disorder in Children: A Receiver Operating Characteristic Curve Analysis." *Bipolar Disorders* 7, no. 6, pp. 518–24. doi:10.1111/j.1399-5618.2005.00271.x

Faulstich, M.E., M.P. Carey, L. Ruggiero, P. Enyart, and F. Gresham. 1986. "Assessment of Depression in Childhood and Adolescence: An Evaluation of the Center for Epidemiological Studies Depression Scale for Children (CES-DC)." *American Journal of Psychiatry* 143, no. 8, pp. 1024–27.

Feeny, N.C., C.K. Danielson, L. Schwartz, E.A. Youngstrom, and R.L. Findling. 2006. "Cognitive-Behavioral Therapy for Bipolar Disorders in Adolescents: A Pilot Study." *Bipolar Disorders* 8, pp. 508–15. doi:10.1111/j.1399-5618.2006.00358.x

Findling, R., R.L. Landbloom, A. Szegedi, J. Koppenhaver, S. Braat, Q. Zhu, and M. Mathews. 2015. "Asenapine for the Acute Treatment of Pediatric Manic or Mixed Episode of Bipolar I Disorder." *Journal of the American Academy of Child & Adolescent Psychiatry* 54, no. 12, pp. 1032–41. doi:10.1016/j.jaac.2015.09.007

Frank, E., D.J. Kupfer, M.E. Thase, A.G. Mallinger, H.A. Swartz, A.M. Fagiolini, and T. Monk. 2005. "Two Year Outcomes for Interpersonal and Social Rhythm Therapy in Individuals with Bipolar I Disorder." *Archives of General Psychiatry* 62, no. 9, pp. 996–1004.

Frazier, E.A., B. Gracious, L.E. Arnold, M. Failla, C. Chitchumroonchokchai, D. Habash, and M.A. Fristad. 2013. "Nutritional and Safety Outcomes from an Open-Label Micronutrient Intervention for Pediatric Bipolar Spectrum Disorders." *Journal of Child and Adolescent Psychopharmacology* 23, no. 8, pp. 558–67. doi:10.1089/cap.2012.0098

Frazier, T.W., C.A. Demeter, E.A. Youngstrom, J.R. Calabrese, R.J. Stansbrey, N.A. McNamara, and R.L. Findling. 2007. "Evaluation and Comparison of Psychometric Instruments for Pediatric Bipolar Spectrum Disorders in Four Age Groups." *Journal of Child and Adolescent Psychopharmacology* 6, no. 17, pp. 853–66. doi:10.1089/cap.2007.0057

Frazier, T.W., E.A. Youngstrom, M.A. Fristad, C. Demeter, B. Birmaher, R.A. Kowatch, and R.L. Findling. 2014. "Improving Clinical Prediction of Bipolar Spectrum Disorders in Youth." *Journal of Clinical Medicine* 3, no. 1, pp. 218–32. doi:10.3390/jcm3010218

Freeman, A.J., E.A. Youngstrom, M.J. Freeman, J.K. Youngstrom, and R.L. Findling. 2011. "Is Caregiver-Adolescent Disagreement Due to Differences in Thresholds for Reporting Manic Symptoms?" *Journal of Child and Adolescent Psychopharmacology* 21, no. 5, pp. 425–32. doi:10.1089/cap.2011.0033

Frías, Á., C. Palma, and N. Farriols. 2014a. "Comorbidity in Pediatric Bipolar Disorder: Prevalence, Clinical Impact, Etiology and Treatment." *Journal of Affective Disorders* 174, pp. 378–89. doi:10.1016/j.jad.2014.12.008

Frías, Á., C. Palma, and N. Farriols. 2014b. "Neurocognitive Impairments Among Youth with Pediatric Bipolar Disorder: A Systematic Review of Neuropsychological Research." *Journal of Affective Disorders* 166, pp. 297–306. doi:10.1016/j.jad.2014.05.025

Frías, Á., C. Palma, and N. Farriols. 2015. "Psychosocial Interventions in the Treatment of Youth Diagnosed or at High-Risk for Pediatric Bipolar Disorder: A Review of the Literature." *Revistade Psiquiatria Salud Mental* (English Edition) 8, no. 3, pp. 146–56. doi:10.1016/j.rpsm.2014.11.002

Fristad, M.A., and G.P. Algorta. 2013. "Future Directions for Research on Youth with Bipolar Spectrum Disorders." *Journal of Clinical Child & Adolescent Psychology* 42, no. 5, pp. 734–47. doi:10.1080/15374416.2013.817312

Fristad, M.A., T.W. Frazier, E.A. Youngstrom, K. Mount, B.W. Fields, C. Demeter, and R.L. Findling. 2012. "What Differentiates Children Visiting Outpatient Mental Health Services with Bipolar Spectrum Disorder from Children with Other Psychiatric Diagnoses?" *Bipolar Disorders* 14, pp. 497–506. doi:10.1111/j.1399-5618.2012.01034.x

Fristad, M.A., and J.S. Goldberg Arnold. 2011a. *Individual-Family Psycho-educational Psychotherapy (IF-PEP): Parent workbook.* Columbus, OH: CFPSI Press.

Fristad, M.A., and J.S. Goldberg Arnold. 2011b. *Multi-Family Psychoeducational Psychotherapy (MF-PEP): Parent Workbook.* Columbus, OH: CFPSI Press.

Fristad, M.A., and H.A. Macpherson. 2014. "Evidence-Based Psychosocial Treatments for Child and Adolescent Bipolar Spectrum Disorders." *Journal of Clinical Child and Adolescent Psychology* 43, pp. 339–55. doi:10.1080/153 74416.2013.822309

Fristad, M.A., J.S. Verducci, K. Walters, and M.E. Young. 2009. "Impact of Multifamily Psychoeducational Psychotherapy in Treating Children Aged 8 to 12 Years with Mood Disorders." *Archives of General Psychiatry* 66, pp. 1013–21. doi:10.1001/archgenpsychiatry.2009.112

Gadow, K.D., and J. Spratkin. 2015. *Child and Adolescent Symptom Inventory–5.* Stony Brook, NY: Checkmate Plus.

Galanter, C.A., S.R. Hundt, P. Goyal, J. Le, and P.W. Fisher. 2012. "Variability Among Research Diagnostic Interview Instruments in the Application of DSM-IV-TR Criteria of Pediatric Bipolar Disorder." *Journal of the American Academy of Child & Adolescent Psychiatry* 51, no. 6, pp. 605–21. doi:10.1016/j. jaac.2012.03.010

Garvey, M., S. Avenevoli, and K. Anderson. 2016. "The National Institute of Mental Health Research Domain Criteria and Clinical Research in Child and Adolescent Psychiatry." *Journey of American Academy of Child and Adolescent Psychiatry* 55, no. 2, pp. 93–98. doi:10.1016/j.jaac.2015. 11.002

Geller, B., M. Williams, B. Zimerman, and J. Frazier. 1996. *Washington University in St. Louis Kiddie Schedule for Affective Disorders and Schizophrenia (WASH-U-KSADS).* St Louis, MO: Washington University.

Geller, B., B. Zimerman, M. Williams, K. Bolhofner, J.L. Craney, M.P. DelBello, and C. Soutullo. 2001. "Reliability of the Washington University in St. Louis Kiddie Schedule for Affective Disorders and Schizophrenia (WASH-U-KSADS) Mania and Rapid Cycling Sections." *Journal of the American Academy of Child & Adolescent Psychiatry* 40, pp. 450–55. doi:10.1097/00004583-200104000-00014

Gershon, A., and M.K. Singh. 2016. "Sleep in Adolescents with Bipolar I Disorder: Stability and Relation to Symptom change." *Journal of Clinical Child & Adolescent Psychology*, pp. 1–11. doi:10.1080/15374416.2016.118 8699

Ghaemi, S.N., C.J. Miller, D.A. Berv, J. Klugman, K.J. Rosenquist, and R.W. Pies. 2005. "Sensitivity and Specificity of a New Bipolar Spectrum Diagnostic Scale." *Journal of Affective Disorders* 84, nos. 2–3, pp. 273–77. doi:10.1016/ S0165-0327(03)00196-4

Gibbons, R.D., C. Brown, K. Hur, J.M. Davis, and J. Mann. 2012. "Suicidal Thoughts and Behavior with Antidepressant Treatment: Reanalysis of the Randomized Placebo-Controlled Studies of Fluoxetine and Venlafaxine." *Archives of General Psychiatry* 69, no. 6, pp. 580–87. doi:10.1001/ archgenpsychiatry.2011.2048.

Gioia, G.A., P.K. Isquith, S.C. Guy, and L. Kenworthy. 2015. *Behavior Rating Inventory of Executive Functioning-Second Edition (BRIEF-2).* Torrance, CA: Western Psychological Services (WPS).

Goetz, M., T. Novak, M. Vesela, Z. Hlavka, M. Brunovsky, M. Povazan, and A. Sebela. 2015. "Early Stages of Pediatric Bipolar Disorder: Retrospective Analysis of a Czech Inpatient Sample." *Neuropsychiatric Disease and Treatment* 11, pp. 2855–64. doi:10.2147/NDT.S79586

Goldstein, T.R., D.A. Axelson, B. Birmaher, and D.A. Brent. 2007. "Dialectical Behavior Therapy for Adolescents with Bipolar Disorder: A One-Year Open Trial." *Journal of the American Academy of Child and Adolescent Psychiatry* 46, no. 7, pp. 820–30. doi:10.1097/chi.0b013e31805c1613

Goldstein, T.R., R. Fersch-Podrat, D.A. Axelson, A. Gilbert, S.A. Hlastala, B. Birmaher, and E. Frank. 2014. "Early Intervention for Adolescents at High Risk for the Development of Bipolar Disorder: Pilot Study of Interpersonal and Social Rhythm Therapy (IPSRT)." *Psychotherapy* 51, no. 1, pp. 180–89. doi:10.1037/a0034396

Goldstein, T.R., R. Fersch-Podrat, M. Rivera, D.A. Axelson, J. Merranko, and B. Birmaher. 2015. "Dialectical Behavior Therapy for Adolescents with Bipolar Disorder: Results from a Pilot Randomized Trial." *Journal of Child and Adolescent Psychopharmacology* 25, no. 2, pp. 140–49. doi:10.1089/cap.2013.0145

Goodman, R., T. Ford, H. Richards, R. Gatward, and H. Meltzer. 2000. "The Development and Well-Being Assessment: Description and Initial Validation of an Integrated Assessment of Child and Adolescent Psychopathology." *Journal of Child Psychology and Psychiatry* 41, pp. 645–55. doi:10.1111/j.1469-7610.2000.tb02345.x

Goodwin, F.K., and K.R. Jamison. 2007. *Manic-depressive illness* 2nd ed. New York: Oxford University Press.

Goodwin, G.M., P.M. Haddad, I.N. Ferrier, J.K. Aronson, T.R.H. Barnes, A. Cipriani, and A. Young. 2016. "Evidence-Based Guidelines for Treating Bipolar Disorder: Revised Third Edition Recommendations from the British Association for Psychopharmacology." *Journal of Psychopharmacology* 30, no. 6, pp. 495–553. doi:10.1177/0269881116636545

Gracious, B.L., E.A. Youngstrom, R.L. Findling, and J.R. Calabrese. 2002. "Discriminative Validity of a Parent Version of the Young Mania Rating Scale." *Journal of the American Academy of Child & Adolescent Psychiatry* 41, pp. 1350–59. doi:10.1097/00004583-200211000-00017

Gruber, J., K. Gilbert, E.A. Youngstrom, J.K. Youngstrom, N.C. Feeny, and R.L. Findling. 2013. "Reward Dysregulation and Mood Symptoms in an Adolescent Outpatient Sample." *Journal of Abnormal Child Psychology* 41, pp. 1053–65. doi:10.1007/s10802-013-9746-8

Hafeman, D., D. Axelson, C. Demeter, R.L. Findling, M.A. Fristad, R.A. Kowatch, and B. Birmaher. 2013. "Phenomenology of Bipolar Disorder not Otherwise Specified in Youth: A Comparison of Clinical Characteristics Across the Spectrum of Manic Symptoms." *Bipolar Disorder* 15, pp. 240–52. doi:10.1111/bdi.12054

Hanmaker, E.L., R.P. Grasman, and J. Henk Kamphuis. 2016. "Modeling BAS Dysregulation in Bipolar Disorder: Illustrating the Potential of Time Series Analysis." *Sage Journals* 23, no. 4, pp. 436–46. doi:10.1177/1073191116632339

Hauser, M., B. Galling, and C.U. Correll. 2013. "Suicidal Ideation and Suicide Attempts in Children and Adolescents with Bipolar Disorder: A Systematic Review of Prevalence and Incidence Rates, Correlates, and Targeted Interventions." *Bipolar Disorder* 15, pp. 507–23. doi:10.1111/bdi.12094

Heiler, S., T. Legenbauer, T. Bogen, T. Jensch, and M. Holtmann. 2011. "Severe Mood Dysregulation: In the 'Light' of Circadian Functioning." *Medical Hypotheses* 77, no. 4, pp. 692–95. doi:10.1016/j.mehy.2011.07.019

Hirneth, S.J., P.L. Hazell, T. Hanstock, and T. Lewin. 2015. "Bipolar Disorder Subtypes in Children and Adolescents: Demographic and Clinical Characteristics from an Australian Sample." *Journal of Affective Disorders* 175, no. 1, pp. 98–107. doi:10.1016/j.jad.2014.12.021

Hirschfeld, R.M., J.B. Williams, R.L. Spitzer, J.R. Calabrese, and L. Flynn. 2000. "Development and Validation of a Screening Instrument for Bipolar Spectrum Disorder: The Mood Disorder Questionnaire." *American Journal of Psychiatry* 157, pp. 1873–75. doi:10.1176/appi.ajp.157.11.1873

Hlastala, S.A., and J. Kotler. 2007. *Treatment Manual for Interpersonal and Social Rhythm Therapy for Adolescent Bipolar Disorder (IPSRT-A).* Unpublished manual.

Hlastala, S.A., J. Kotler, J. McClellan, and E. McCauley. 2010. "Interpersonal and Social Rhythm Therapy for Adolescents with Bipolar Disorder: Treatment Development and Results from an Open Trial." *Depression and Anxiety* 27, pp. 457–64. doi:10.1002/da.20668

Holtmann, M., F. Pörtner, E. Duketis, H.H. Flechtner, J. Angst, and G. Lehmkuhl. 2009. "Validation of the Hypomania Checklist (HCL-32) in a Nonclinical Sample of German Adolescents." *Journal of Adolescence* 32, no. 5, pp. 1075–88. doi:10.1016/j.adolescence.2009.03.004

Holtzman, J.N., S. Miller, F. Hooshmand, P.W. Wang, K.D. Chang, S.J. Hill, and T.A. Ketter. 2015. "Childhood-Compared to Adolescent-Onset Bipolar Disorder Has More Statistically Significant Clinical Correlates." *Journal of Affective Disorders* 179, pp. 114–20. doi:10.1016/j.jad.2015.03.019

Jenkins, M., E. Youngstrom, J. Washburn, and J. Youngstrom. 2011. "Evidence-Based Strategies Improve Assessment of Pediatric Bipolar Disorder by Community Practitioners." *Professional Psychology: Research & Practice* 42, no. 2, pp. 121–29. doi:10.1037/a0022506

Jenkins, M.M., E.A. Youngstrom, J.K. Youngstrom, C. Feeny, and R.L. Findling. 2012. "Generalizability of Evidence-Based Assessment Recommendations for Pediatric Bipolar Disorder." *Psychological Assessment* 24, pp. 269–81. doi:10.1037/a0025775

Joshi, G., and T. Wilens. 2015. "Comorbid Conditions in Youth with and at Risk for Bipolar Disorder." In *Bipolar Disorder in Youth: Presentation, Treatment, & Neurobiology*, eds. S.M. Strakowski, M.P. DelBello, and C.M. Adler, pp. 56–93. New York: Oxford University Press.

Joslyn, C., D.J. Hawes, C. Hunt, and P.B. Mitchell. 2016. "Is Age of Onset Associated with Severity, Prognosis, and Clinical Features in Bipolar Disorder? A Meta-Analytic Review." *Bipolar Disorders*, pp. 1–15. doi:10.1111/bdi.12419

Kamphaus, R.W., and C.R. Reynolds. 2007. *Behavior Assessment System for Children, 2nd ed (BASC-2)*. Bloomington, MN: Pearson Publishing.

Keenan-Miller, D., and D.J. Miklowitz. 2011. "Interpersonal Functioning in Pediatric Bipolar Disorder." *Clinical Psychology Science and Practice* 18, no. 4, pp. 342–56. doi:10.1111/j.1468-2850.2011.01266.x

Keenan-Miller, D., T. Peris, D. Axelson, R.A. Kowatch, and D.J. Miklowitz. 2012. "Family Functioning, Social Impairment, and Symptoms Among Adolescents with Bipolar Disorder." *Journal of the American Academy of Child & Adolescent Psychiatry* 51, no. 10, pp. 1085–94. doi:10.1016/j.jaac.2012.08.005

Kennedy, K.P., K.R. Cullen, C.G. DeYoung, and B. Klimes-Dougan. 2015. "The Genetics of Early-Onset Bipolar Disorder: A Systematic Review." *Journal of Affective Disorders* 184, pp. 1–12. doi:10.1016/j.jad.2015.05.017

Kessing, L., E. Vradi, and P. Andersen. 2015. "Diagnostic Stability in Pediatric Bipolar Disorder." *Journal of Affective Disorders* 172, pp. 417–21. doi:10.1016/j.jad.2014.10.037

Khazanov, G.K., L. Cui, K.R. Merikangas, and J. Angst. 2015. "Treatment Patterns of Youth with Bipolar Disorder: Results from the National Comorbidity Survey—Adolescent Supplement (NCS-A)." *Journal of Abnormal Child Psychology* 43, pp. 391–400. doi:10.1007/s10802-014-9885-6

Kim, K.L., A.B. Weissman, M.E. Puzia, G.K. Cushman, K.E. Seymour, E. Wegbreit, D.P. Dickstein. 2014. "Circadian Phase Preference in Pediatric Bipolar Disorder." *Journal of Clinical Medicine* 3, no. 1, pp. 255–66. doi:10.3390/jcm30102550

Klaus, N., G. Algorta, A. Young, and M. Fristad. 2015. "Validity of the Expressed Emotion Adjective Checklist (EEAC) in Caregivers of Children with Mood Disorders." *Couple and Family Psychology: Research and Practice* 4, no. 1, pp. 27–38. doi:10.1037/cfp0000036

Koenen, K.C., T.E. Moffitt, A.L. Roberts, L. Martin, L. Kubzansky, H. Harrington, and A. Caspi. 2009. "Childhood IQ and Adult Mental Disorders: A Test of the Cognitive Reserve Hypothesis." *The American Journal of Psychiatry* 166, no. 1, pp. 50–57. Retrieved from https://georgefox.idm.oclc.org/login?url=http://search.proquest.com.georgefox.idm.oclc.org/docview/220465540?accountid=11085

Kowatch, R.A., M.A. Fristad, R.L. Findling, and R.M. Post. 2009. *Clinical Manual for Management of Bipolar Disorder in Children and Adolescents.* Arlington, VA: American Psychiatric Publishing.

Kowatch, R.A., E.A. Youngstrom, S. Horwitz, C. Demeter, M.A. Fristad, B. Birmaher, R.L. Findling. 2013. "Prescription of Psychiatric Medications and Polypharmacy in the LAMS Cohort." *Psychiatric Services* 64, no. 10, pp. 1026–34. Retrieved from https://georgefox.idm.oclc.org/login?url=http://search.proquest.com/docview/1444011879?accountid=11085

Lagace, D.C., S.P. Kutcher. 2005. "Academic Performance of Adolescents with Bipolar Disorder." *Directions in Psychiatry* 25, pp. 111–17.

Lee, M.-S., P. Anumagalla, P. Talluri, and M.N. Pavuluri. 2014. "Meta-Analyses of Developing Brain Function in High-Risk and Emerged Bipolar Disorder." *Frontiers in Psychiatry* 5, p. 141. doi:10.3389/fpsyt.2014.00141

Lera-Miguel, S., S. Andrés-Perpiñá, M. Fatjó-Vilas, L. Fañanás, and L. Lázaro. 2015. "Two-Year Follow-Up of Treated Adolescents with Early-Onset Bipolar Disorder: Changes in Neurocognition." *Journal of Affective Disorders* 172, pp. 48–54. doi:10.1016/j.jad.2014.09.041

Liang, J., B. Matheson, and J.M. Douglas. 2016. "Mental Health Diagnostic Considerations in Racial/Ethnic Minority Youth." *Journal of Child & Family Studies* 25, pp. 1926–40. doi:10.1007/s10826-015-0351-z

Lichtenstein, P., B.H. Yip, C. Björk, Y. Pawitan, T.D. Cannon, P.F. Sullivan, and C.M. Hultman. 2009. "Common Genetic Determinants of Schizophrenia and Bipolar Disorder in Swedish Families: A Population-Based Study." *The Lancet* 373, no. 9659, pp. 234–39. http://dx.doi.org.georgefox.idm.oclc.org/10.1016/S0140-6736(09)60072-6

Linehan, M. 1993. *Cognitive-Behavioral Treatment of Borderline Personality Disorder.* New York, NY: Guilford Press.

Lunsford-Avery, J.R., C.M. Judd, D.A. Axelson, and D.J. Miklowitz. 2012. "Sleep Impairment, Mood Symptoms, and Psychosocial Functioning in Adolescent Bipolar Disorder." *Psychiatry Research* 200, nos. 2–3, pp. 265–71. doi:10.1016/j.psychres.2012.07.037

Lytle, S.M., S.K. Moratschek, and R.L. Findling. 2015. "Medical Treatment Strategies for Young People with Bipolar Disorder." In *Bipolar Disorder in Youth: Presentation, Treatment, & Neurobiology,* eds. S.M. Strakowski, M.P. DelBello, and C.M. Adler, pp. 156–88. New York, NY: Oxford University Press.

MacCabe, J.H., M.P. Lambe, S. Cnattingius, P.C. Sham, A.S. David, A. Reichenberg, and C.M. Hultman. 2010. "Excellent School Performance at Age 16 and Risk of Adult Bipolar Disorder: National Cohort Study." *British Journal of Psychiatry* 196, pp. 109–15. doi:10.1192/bjp.bp.108.060368 20118454

MacPherson, H.A., J.M. Leffler, and M.A. Fristad. 2014. "Implementation of Multi-Family Psychoeducational Psychotherapy for Childhood Mood Disorders in an Outpatient Community Setting." *Journal of Marital & Family Therapy* 40, no. 2, pp. 193–211. doi:10.1111/jmft.12013

Mahon, K., K. Burdick, and A. Malhotra. 2015. "Heritability of Bipolar Disorder." In *Bipolar Disorder in Youth: Presentation, Treatment, & Neurobiology*, eds. S.M. Strakowski, M.P. DelBello, and C.M. Adler, pp. 94–108. New York: Oxford University Press.

Maniglio, R. 2013a. "The Impact of Child Sexual Abuse on the Course of Bipolar Disorder: A Systematic Review." *Bipolar Disorders* 15, no. 4, pp. 341–58. doi:10.1111/bdi.12050

Maniglio, R. 2013b. "Prevalence of Child Sexual Abuse Among Adults and Youths with Bipolar Disorder: A Systematic Review." *Clinical Psychology Review* 33, pp. 561–73. doi:10.1016/j.cpr.2013.03.002

Marangoni, C., M. Hernandez, and G.L. Faedda. 2016. "The Role of Environmental Exposures as Risk Factors for Bipolar Disorder: A Systematic Review of Longitudinal Studies." *Journal of Affective Disorders* 193, pp. 165–174. doi:10.1016/j.jad.2015.12.055

McCarthy, J.B., S.R. Weiss, K.T. Segovich, and B. Barbot. 2016. "Impact of Psychotic Symptoms on Cognitive Functioning in Child and Adolescent Psychiatric Inpatients with Severe Mood Disorders." *Psychiatry Research* 244, pp. 223–28. doi:10.1016/j.psychres.2016.07.049

McClellan, J., R. Kowatch, and R.L. Findling. 2007. "Practice Parameter for the Assessment and Treatment of Children and Adolescents with Bipolar Disorder." *Journal of the American Academy of Child & Adolescent Psychiatry* 46, no. 1, pp. 107–25. doi:10.1097/01.chi.0000242240.69678.c4

McNamara, R.K., and J.R. Strawn. 2015. "Nonheritable Risk Factors for Bipolar Disorder." In *Bipolar Disorder in Youth: Presentation, Treatment, & Neurobiology*, eds. S.M. Strakowski, M.P. DelBello, C.M. and Adler, pp. 109–132. New York, NY: Oxford Press.

Merikangas, K.R., L.H. Cui, G. Kattan, G.A. Carlson, E.A. Youngstrom, and J. Angst. 2012. "Mania with and without Depression in a Community Sample of US Adolescents." *Archives of General Psychiatry* 69, pp. 943–51. doi:10.1001/archgenpsychiatry.2012.38

Merikangas, K.R., R. Jin, J.P. He, R.C. Kessler, S. Lee, N.A. Sampson, and Z. Zarkov. 2011. "Prevalence and Correlates of Bipolar Spectrum Disorder in the World Mental Health Survey Initiative." *Archives of General Psychiatry* 68, pp. 241–51. doi:10.1001/archgenpsychiatry.2011.12

Metcalfe, A.W., B.J. MacIntosh, A. Scavone, X. Ou, and B.I. Goldstein. 2016. "Effects of Acute Aerobic Exercise on Neural Correlates of Attention and Inhibition in Adolescents with Bipolar Disorder." *Translational Psychiatry* 6, no. 5, p. e814. doi:10.1038/tp.2016.85

Meyer, S.E., G.A. Carlson, E. Youngstrom, D.S. Ronsaville, P.E. Martinez, R. Gold, and M. Radke-Yarrow. 2009. "Long-Term Outcomes of Youth who Manifested the CBCL-Pediatric Bipolar Disorder Phenotype During Childhood and/or Adolescence." *Journal of Affective Disorders* 113, pp. 227–35. doi:10.1016/j.jad.2008.05.024

Miguez, M., B. Weber, M. Debbane, D. Balanzin, M. Gex-Fabry, F. Raiola, and J.M. Aubry. 2013. "Screening for Bipolar Disorder in Adolescents with the Mood Disorder Questionnaire - Adolescent Version (MDQ-A) and the Child Bipolar Questionnaire (CBQ)." *Early Interventions in Psychiatry* 7, pp. 270–77. doi:10.1111/j.1751-7893.2012.00388.x

Miklowitz, D.J. 2010. *Bipolar Disorder: A Family-Focused Treatment Approach.* New York, NY: Guilford Press.

Miklowitz, D.J., D.A. Axelson, B. Birmaher, E.L. George, D.O. Taylor, C.D. Schneck, and D.A. Brent. 2008. "Family-Focused Treatment for Adolescents with Bipolar Disorder: Results of a 2-year Randomized Trial." *Archives of General Psychiatry* 65, no. 9, pp. 1053–61. doi:10.1001/archpsyc.65.9.1053

Miklowitz, D.J., D.A. Axelson, E.L. George, D.O. Taylor, C.D. Schneck, A.E. Sullivan, and B. Birmaher. 2009. "Expressed Emotion Moderates the Effects of Family-Focused Treatment for Bipolar Adolescents." *Journal of the American Academy of Child & Adolescent Psychiatry* 48, no. 6, pp. 643–51. doi:10.1097/CHI.0b013e3181a0ab9d

Miklowitz, D.J., M.P. O'Brien, D.A. Schlosser, J.L. Zinberg, S. De Silva, E.L. George, and T.D. Cannon. 2012. *Clinicians' Treatment Manual for Family-Focused Therapy for Early-Onset Youth and Young Adults (FFT-EOY).* Retrieved from http://www.semel.ucla.edu/champ/downloads-clinicians.

Miklowitz, D.J., C.D. Schneck, E.L. George, D.O. Taylor, C.A. Sugar, B. Birmaher, and D. Axelson. 2014. "Pharmacotherapy and Family-Focused Treatment for Adolescents with Bipolar I and II Disorders: A 2-year Randomized Trial." *American Journal of Psychiatry* 171, no. 6, pp. 658–67. doi:10.1176/appi.ajp.2014.13081130

Miklowitz, D.J., C.D. Schneck, M.K. Singh, D.O. Taylor, E.L. George, V.E. Cosgrove, and K.D. Chang. 2013. "Early Intervention for Symptomatic Youth at Risk for Bipolar Disorder: A Randomized Trial of Family Focused Therapy." *Journal of the American Academy of Child & Adolescent Psychiatry* 52, no. 2, pp. 121–31. doi:10.1016/j.jaac.2012.10.007

Muroff, J., G.A. Edelsohn, S. Joe, and B.C. Ford. 2008. "The Role of Race in Diagnostic and Disposition Decision Making in a Pediatric Psychiatric Emergency Service." *General Hospital Psychiatry* 30, pp. 269–76. doi:10.1016/j.genhosppsych.2008.01.003

Mwangi, B., D. Spiker, G. Zunta-Soares, and J. Soares. 2014. "Prediction of Pediatric Bipolar Disorder Using Neuroanatomical Signatures of the Amygdala." *Bipolar Disorders* 16, no. 7, pp. 713–21. doi:10.1111/bdi.12222

Nader, E.G., A. Kleinman, B. Carramao Gomes, C., Bruscagin, B. dos Santos, M., Nicoletti, and S.C. Caetano. 2013. "Negative Expressed Emotion Best Discriminates Families with Bipolar Disorder Children." *Journal of Affective Disorders* 148, pp. 418–23. doi:10.1016/j.jad.2012.11.017

National Institute for Health and Clinical Excellence. 2016. "Bipolar Disorder: The Management of Bipolar Disorder in Adults, Children and Adolescents in Primary and Secondary Care." *Clinical Guideline* 185. London: NICE.

National Institute of Mental Health (n.d.). Retrieved July 1, 2016 from http://www.nimh.nih.gov/about/index.shtml   http://neurowiki2013.wikidot.com/group:bipolar-neuroscience

Nieto, R., and F.A. Castellanos. 2011. "Meta-Analysis of Neuropsychological Functioning in Patients with Early Onset Schizophrenia and Pediatric Bipolar Disorder." *Journal of Clinical Child & Adolescent Psychology* 40, no. 2, pp. 266–80. doi:10.1080/15374416.2011.546049

Nurnberger, J.I., D.L. Koller, J. Jung, H.J. Edenberg, T. Foroud, I. Guella, J.R. Kelsoe. 2014. "Identification of Pathways for Bipolar Disorder: A Meta-Analysis." *JAMA Psychiatry* 71, no. 6, pp. 657–64. doi:10.1001/jamapsychiatry.2014.176

Papachristou, E., J. Ormel, A.J. Oldehinkel, M. Kyriakopoulos, M. Reinares, A. Reichenberg, and S. Frangou. 2013. "Child Behavior Checklist - Mania Scale (CBCL-MS): Development and Evaluation of a Population-Based Screening Scale for Bipolar Disorder." *PLoS ONE* 8, no. 8. doi:10.1371/journal.pone.0069459

Papolos, D., J. Hennen, M.S. Cockerham, H.C. Thode, and E.A. Youngstrom. 2006. "The Child Bipolar Questionnaire: A Dimensional Approach to Screening for Pediatric Bipolar Disorder." *Journal of Affective Disorders* 95, pp. 149–58. doi:10.1016/j.jad.2006.03.026

Papolos, D. (undated). *The Jeannie and Jeffrey Illustrated Interview for Children.* www.jbrf.org/the-jeannie-jeffrey-illustrated-interview-for-children/

Pavuluri, M.N., D.B. Henry, B. Devineni, J.A. Carbray and B. Birmaher. 2006. "Child Mania Rating Scale: Development, Reliability, and Validity." *Journal of the American Academy of Child & Adolescent Psychiatry* 45, pp. 550–60. doi:10.1097/01.chi.0000205700.40700.50

Pavuluri, M., and A. May. 2014. "Differential Treatment of Pediatric Bipolar Disorder and Attention-Deficit/Hyperactivity Disorder." *Psychiatric Annals* 44, no. 10, pp. 471–80. doi:http://dx.doi.org.georgefox.idm.oclc.org/10.3928/00485713-20141003-06

Pavuluri, M.N., A.M. Passarotti, T. Mohammed, J.A. Carbray, and J.A. Sweeney. 2010. "Enhanced Working and Verbal Memory After Lamotrigine Treatment in Pediatric Bipolar Disorder." *Bipolar Disorders* 12, pp. 213–20. doi:10.1111/j.13995618.2010.00792.x

Pendergast, L.L., E.A. Youngstrom, C. Brong, D. Jensen, L. Abramson, and L.B. Alloy. 2015. "Structural Invariance of General Behavior Inventory (GBI) Scores in Black and White Young Adults." *Psychological Assessment* 27, no. 1, pp. 21–30. doi:10.1037/pas0000020

Perlman, S.B., J.C. Fournier, G., Bebko, M.A. Bertocci, A.K. Hinze, L. Bonar, and L.E. Arnold. 2013. "Emotional Face Processing in Pediatric Bipolar Disorder: Evidence for Functional Impairments in the Fusiform Gyrus." *Journal of the American Academy of Child & Adolescent Psychiatry* 52, no. 12, pp. 1314–25. doi:10.1016/j.jaac.2013.09.004

Peters, A.T., D.B. Henry, and A.E. West. 2015. "Caregiver Characteristics and Symptoms of Pediatric Bipolar Disorder." *Journal of Child and Family Studies* 24, no. 5, pp. 1469–80. doi:http://dx.doi.org.georgefox.idm.oclc.org/10.1007/s10826-014-9952-1

Posner, K., G.K. Brown, B. Stanley, D.A. Brent, K.V. Yershova, M.A. Oquendo, and J.J. Mann. 2011. "The Columbia-Suicide Severity Rating Scale: Initial Validity and Internal Consistency Findings from Three Multisite Studies with Adolescents and Adults." *American Journal of Psychiatry* 168, pp. 1266–77.

Post, R.M., L.L. Altshuler, R. Kupka, S.L. McElroy, M.A. Frye, M. Rowe, and W.A. Nolen. 2015. "Verbal Abuse, Like Physical and Sexual Abuse, in Childhood is Associated with an Earlier Onset and More Difficult Course of Bipolar Disorder." *Bipolar Disorders* 17, pp. 323–30. doi:10.1111/bdi.12268

Post, R.M., L.L. Altshuler, R. Kupka, S. McElroy, M.A. Fryer, M. Rowe, and W. Nolen. 2016. "Age of Onset of Bipolar Disorder: Combined Effect of Childhood Adversity and Familial Loading of Psychiatric Disorders." *Journal of Psychiatric Research* 81, pp. 63–70. doi:10.1016/j.jpsychires.2016.06.008

Post, R.M., R.L., Findling, and D.A. Luckenbaugh. 2014. "Number, Severity, and Quality of Symptoms Discriminate Early-Onset Bipolar Disorder from Attention-Deficit/Hyperactivity Disorder." *Psychiatric Annals* 44, no. 9, pp. 416–22. doi:http://dx.doi.org.georgefox.idm.oclc.org/10.3928/00485713-20140908-05

Poznanski, E.O., L.N. Freeman, and H.B. Mokros. 1985. "Children's Depression Rating Scale-Revised." *Psychopharmacology Bulletin* 21, pp. 979–89.

Propper, L., A. Ortiz, C. Slaney, J. Garnham, M. Ruzickova, C.V. Calkin, and M. Alda. 2015. "Early-Onset and Very-Early-Onset Bipolar Disorder: Distinct or Similar Clinical Conditions?" *Bipolar Disorders* 17, pp. 814–20.

Rajakannan, T., J.M. Zito, M. Burcu, and D.J. Safer. 2014. "Pediatric Bipolar Disorder: Subtype Trend and Impact of Behavioral Comorbidities." *Journal of Clinical Medicine* 3, pp. 310–22. doi:10.3390/jcm3010310

Ratheesh, A., M. Berk, C. Davey, P.D. McGorry, and S.M. Cotton. 2015. "Instruments that Prospectively Predict Bipolar Disorder—A Systematic Review." *Journal of Affective Disorders* 179, pp. 65–73. doi:10.1016/j.jad.2015.03.025

Rathus, J., and A. Miller. 2015. *DBT^R Skills Manual for Adolescents*. New York, NY: Guilford Press.

Ravens-Sieberer, U., and M. Bullinger. 2000. *KINDL: Questionnaire for Measuring Health Related Quality of Life in Children and Adolescents, Revised version. Manual*. KINDL, Berlin, Germany.

Reichart, C.G., J. van der Ende, M. Wals, M.H. Hillegers, W.A. Nolen, J. Ormel, and F.C.Verhulst. 2005. "The Use of the GBI as a Predictor of Bipolar Disorder in a Population of Adolescent Offspring of Parents with a Bipolar Disorder." *Journal of Affective Disorders* 89, nos. 1–3, pp.147–55.

Reynolds, C.R., and R.W. Kamphaus. 2015. *Behavior Assessment System for Children, 3rd ed (BASC-3)*. Bloomington, MN: Pearson Publishing.

Reynolds, W. 1988. *Suicidal Ideation Questionnaire: Professional Manual*. Odessa, FL: Psychological Assessment Resources.

Rich, B.A., S.J. Fromm, L.H. Berghorst, D.P. Dickstein, M.A. Brotman, D.S. Pine, and E. Leibenluft. 2008. "Neural Connectivity in Children with Bipolar Disorder: Impairment in the Face Emotion Processing Circuit." *Journal of Child Psychology & Psychiatry* 49, pp. 88–96. doi:10.1111/j.1469-7610.2007.01819.x

Rich, B.A., T. Holroyd, F.W. Carver, L.M. Onelio, J.K. Mendoza, B.R. Cornwell, and E. Leibenluft. 2010. "A Preliminary Study of the Neural Mechanisms of Frustration in Pediatric Bipolar Disorder Using Magnetoencephalography." *Depression and Anxiety* 27, no. 3, pp. 276–86. doi:10.1002/da.20649

Rizvi, S.H., M. Ong, and E.A. Youngstrom. 2014. "Bipolar Disorder in Children and Adolescents: An Update on Diagnosis." *Clinical Practice* 11, no. 6, pp. 665–76. doi:10.2217/cpr.14.76

Roberts, C., B. Bishop, and R. Rooney. 2008. "Depression and Bipolar Disorder in Childhood." In *Handbook of Childhood Behavioral Issues: Evidence-Based Approaches to Prevention and Treatment*, eds. T.P. Gullotta and G.M. Blau, pp. 239–71. New York, NY: Routledge Press.

Rocher Schudlich, T., E. Youngstrom, M. Martinez, J. KogosYoungstrom, K. Scovil, J. Ross, R. Findling. 2015. "Physical and Sexual Abuse and Early-Onset Bipolar Disorder in Youths Receiving Outpatient Services: Frequent, but not Specific." *Journal of Abnormal Child Psychology* 43, no. 3, pp. 453–463. doi:10.1007/s10802-014-9924-3

Rolim-Neto, M.L., E.A. Silva, A.G. Junior, J. Cartaxo, N.M. Lima, V.B. Nascimento, and P.J. Neto. 2015. "Bipolar Disorder Incidence Between Children and Adolescents: A Brief Communication." *Journal of Affective Disorders* 172, pp. 171–74. doi:10.1016/jad.2014.09.045.

Russo, J.M., S.M. de Zwarte, and H.P. Blumberg. 2015. "Neurobiology of Developing Bipolar Disorder." In *Bipolar Disorder in Youth: Presentation,*

Treatment, & Neurobiology, eds. S.M. Strakowski, M.P. DelBello, and C.M. Adler, pp. 243–81. New York, NY: Oxford University Press.

Schenkel, L.S., T.F. Chamberlain, and T.L. Towne. 2014. "Impaired Theory of Mind and Psychosocial Functioning Among Pediatric Patients with Type I versus Type II Bipolar Disorder." *Psychiatry Research* 215, no. 3, pp. 740–6. doi:10.1016/j.psychres.2013.10.025.

Schenkel, LS., A.E. West, R. Jacobs, J.A. Sweeney, and M.N. Pavluri. 2012. "Cognitive Dysfunction is Worse Among Pediatric Patients with Bipolar Disorder Type I than Type II." *Journal of Child Psychology and Psychiatry* 53, no. 7, pp. 775–81. doi:10.1111/j.1469-7610.2011.02519.x

Schoeyen, H.K., A.B. Birkenaes, A.E. Vaaler, B.H. Auestad, U.F. Malt, O.A. Andreassen, and G. Morken. 2011. "Bipolar Disorder Patients have Similar Levels of Education but Lower Socio-Economic Status than the General Population." *Journal of Affective Disorders* 129, pp. 68–74. doi:10.1016/j.jad.2010.08.012

Schrank, F.A., N. Mather, and K.S. McGrew. 2014. *Woodcock-Johnson IV Tests of Cognitive Abilities Examiner's Manual, Standard and Extended Batteries.* Rolling Meadows, IL: Riverside Publishing.

Schrank, F.A., K.S. McGrew, N. Mather, and R.W. Woodcock. 2014. *Woodcock-Johnson IV Tests of Achievement (WJ IV-ACH).* Rolling Meadows, IL: Riverside Publishing.

Serafini, G., M. Pompili, S. Borgwardt, J. Houenou, P.A. Geoffroy, R. Jardri, and M. Amore. 2014. "Brain Changes in Early-Onset Bipolar and Unipolar Depressive Disorders: A Systematic Review in Children and Adolescents." *European Child & Adolescent Psychiatry* 23, no. 11, pp. 1023–41. doi: 10.1007/s00787-014-0614-z

Seymour, K.E., M.F. Pescosolido, B.L. Reidy, T.G. Galvan, K.L. Kim, M. Young, and D.P. Dickstein. 2013. "Emotional Face Identification in Youths with Primary Bipolar Disorder or Primary Attention-Deficit/Hyperactivity Disorder." *Journal of the American Academy of Child & Adolescent Psychiatry* 52, no. 5, pp. 537–46. doi:10.1016/j.jaac.2013.03.011

Shapiro, J., V.E. Timmins, B. Swampillai, A. Scavone, K. Collinger, C. Boulos, and B.I. Goldstein. 2014. "Correlates of Psychiatric Hospitalization in a Sample of Canadian Adolescents with Bipolar Disorder." *Comprehensive Psychiatry* 55, no. 8, pp. 1855–61. doi:10.1016/j.comppsych.2014.08.048

Siegel, R., A. Freeman, A. La Greca, and E. Youngstrom. 2015a. "Peer Relationship Difficulties in Adolescents with Bipolar Disorder." *Child & Youth Care Forum* 44, no. 3, pp. 355–75. doi:10.1007/s10566-014-9291-9

Siegel, R.S., B. Hoeppner, S. Yen, R.L. Stout, L.M. Weinstock, H.M. Hower, and M.B. Keller. 2015b. "Longitudinal Associations Between Interpersonal Relationship Functioning and Mood Episode Severity in Youth with Bipolar Disorder." *Journal of Nervous & Mental Disease* 203, no. 3, pp. 194–204. doi: 10.1097/NMD.0000000000000261

Simon, D. 2016. Pediatric Bipolar Disorder. In *School-Centered Interventions: Evidence-Based Strategies for Social, Emotional and Academic Success.* Washington, DC: APA.

Singh, M.K., R.G. Kelley, K.D. Chang, and I.H. Gotlib. 2015. "Intrinsic Amygdala Functional Connectivity in Youth with Bipolar I Disorder." *Journal of the American Academy of Child& Adolescent Psychiatry* 54, no. 9, pp. 763–70. doi:10.1016/j.jaac.2015.06.016

Smith, D.J., J. Anderson, S. Zammit, T.D. Meyer, J.P. Pell, and D. MacKay. 2015. "Childhood IQ and Risk of Bipolar Disorder in Adulthood: Prospective Birth Cohort Study." *British Journal of Psychiatry Open* 1, pp. 74–80. doi:10.1192/bjpo.bp. 115.000455

Southam-Gerow, M. 2013. *Emotion Regulation in Children and Adolescents: A Practitioner's Guide.* New York, NY: Guilford Press.

Southammakosane, C., A. Danielyan, J.A. Welge, T.J. Blom, C.M. Adler, K.D. Chang, and M.P. DelBello. 2013. "Characteristics of the Child Behavior Checklist in Adolescents with Depression Associated with Bipolar Disorder." *Journal of Affective Disorders* 145, pp. 405–08. doi:10.1016/j.jad.2012.06.017

Stringaris, A., N. Castellanos-Ryan, T. Banaschewski, G.J. Barker, A.L. Bokde, U. Bromberg, and the Imagen Consortium. 2014. "Dimensions of Manic Symptoms in Youth: Psychosocial Impairment and Cognitive Performance in the IMAGEN Sample." *Journal of Child Psychology & Psychiatry* 55, no. 12, pp. 1380–89. doi:10.1111/jcpp.12255

Sullivan, A.E., C.M. Judd, D.A. Axelson, and D.J. Miklowitz. 2012. "Family Functioning and the Course of Adolescent Bipolar Disorder." *Behavior Therapy* 43, no. 4, pp. 837–47. doi:10.1016/j.beth.2012.04.005

Tillman, R., B. Geller, T. Klages, M. Corrigan, K. Bolhofner, and B. Zimerman. 2008. "Psychotic Phenomena in 257 Young Children and Adolescents with Bipolar I Disorder: Delusions and Hallucinations (Benign and Pathological)." *Bipolar Disorders* 10, pp. 45–55. doi:10.1111/j.1399-5618.2008.00480.x

Timmins, V., B. Swampillai, J. Hatch, A. Scavone, K. Collinger, C. Boulos, and B. Goldstein. 2016. "Correlates of Adolescent-Reported and Parent-Reported Family Conflict Among Canadian Adolescents with Bipolar Disorder." *Journal of Psychiatric Practice* 22, no. 1, pp. 31–41.

Topor, D.R., L. Swenson, J.I. Hunt, B. Birmaher, M. Strober, S. Yen, and M. Keller. 2013. "Manic Symptoms in Youth with Bipolar Disorder: Factor Analysis by Age of Symptom Onset and Current Age." *Journal of Affective Disorder* 145, no. 3, pp. 409–12. doi:10.1016/j.jad.2012.06.024

Toteja, N., P. Guvenek-Cokol, T. Ikuta, V. Kafantaris, B.D. Peters, K.E. Burdick, and P.R. Szeszko. 2015. "Age-Associated Alterations in Corpus Callosum White Matter Integrity in Bipolar Disorder Assessed Using Probabilistic Tractography." *Bipolar Disorders* [serial online] 17, no. 4, pp. 381–91. doi:10.1111/bdi.12278

Tseng, W.L., A.E. Guyer, M.J. Briggs-Gowan, D. Axelson, B. Birmaher, H.L. Egger, and M.A. Brotman. 2015. "Behavior and Emotion Modulation Deficits in Preschoolers at Risk for Bipolar Disorder." *Depression & Anxiety* 32, no. 5, pp. 325–34. doi:10.1002/da.22342

Uchida, M., S.V. Faraone, M. Martelon, T. Kenworthy, K.Y. Woodworth, J.R. Spencer, and J. Biederman. 2015. "Further Evidence that Severe Scores in the Aggression/Anxiety-Depression/Attention Subscales of Child Behavior Checklist (Severe Dysregulation Profile) Can Screen for Bipolar Disorder Symptomatology: A Conditional Probability Analysis." *Journal of Affective Disorders* 165, pp. 81–86. doi:10.1016/j.jad.2014.04.021

Udal, A.H., B. Øygarden, J. Egeland, U.F. Malt, H. Løvdahl, A.H. Pripp, and B. Groholt. 2013. "Executive Deficits in Early Onset Bipolar Disorder Versus ADHD: Impact of Processing Speed and Lifetime Psychosis." *Clinical Child Psychology & Psychiatry* 18, pp. 284–99. doi.org.georgefox.idm.oclc.org/10.1177/1359104512455181

Urosevic, S., E.A. Youngstrom, P. Collins, J. Jensen, and M. Luciana. 2016. "Associations of Age with Reward Delay Discounting and Response Inhibition in Adolescents with Bipolar Disorders." *Journal of Affective Disorders* 190, pp. 649–56. doi:10.1016/j.jad.2015.11.005

Van Meter, A.R., C. Burke, R.A. Kowatch, R.L. Findling, and E.A. Youngstrom. 2016a. "Ten-Year Updated Meta-Analysis of the Clinical Characteristics of Pediatric Mania and Hypomania." *Bipolar Disorders* 18, pp. 19–32. doi:10.1111/bdi.12358

Van Meter, A.R., C. Burke, E.A. Youngstrom, G. Faedda, and C.U. Correll. 2016b. "The Bipolar Prodrome: Meta-Analysis of Symptom Prevalence Prior to Initial or Recurrent Mood Episodes." *Journal of the American Academy of Child & Adolescent* 55, no. 7, pp. 543–55. doi:10.1016/j.jaac.2016.04.017

Van Meter, A.R., A.L. Moreira, and E.A. Youngstrom. 2011. "Meta-Analysis of Epidemiologic Studies of Pediatric Bipolar Disorder." *Journal of Clinical Psychiatry* 72, pp. 1250–56. doi:10.4088/JCP.10m06290

Van Meter, A.R., and E.A. Youngstrom. 2012. "Cyclothymic Disorder in Youth: Why Is It Overlooked, What Do We Know and Where Is the Field Headed?" *Neuropsychiatry* 2, no. 6, pp. 509–10. doi:10.2217/npy.12.64

Van Meter, A., E.A. Youngstrom, C. Demeter, and R.L. Findling. 2013. "Examining the Validity of Cyclothymic Disorder in a Youth Sample: Replication and Extension." *Journal of Abnormal Child Psychology* 41, no. 3, pp. 367–78. doi:10.1007/s10802-012-9680-1

Van Meter, A., E. Youngstrom, A. Freeman, N. Feeny, J.K. Youngstrom, and R.L. Findling. 2016c. "Impact of Irritability and Impulsive Aggressive Behavior on Impairment and Social Functioning in Youth with Cyclothymic Disorder." *Journal of Children and Adolescent Psychopharmacology* 26, no. 1, pp. 26–37. doi:10.1089/cap.2015.0111.

Vande Voort, J.L., A. Singh, J. Bernardi, C. Wall, C.C. Swintak, K.M. Schak, and P.S. Jensen. 2016. "Treatments and Services Provided to Children Diagnosed with Bipolar Disorder." *Child Psychiatry & Human Development* 47, no. 3, pp. 494–502. doi:10.1007/s10578-015-0582-7

Wagner, K.D., R.M. Hirschfeld, G.J. Emslie, R.L. Findling, B.L. Gracious, and M.L. Reed. 2006. "Validation of the Mood Disorder Questionnaire for Bipolar Disorders in Adolescents." *Journal of Clinical Psychiatry* 67, no. 5, pp. 827–830.

Walshaw, P.D., L.B. Alloy, and F.W. Sabb. 2010. "Executive Function in Pediatric Bipolar Disorder and Attention-Deficit Hyperactivity Disorder: In Search of Distinct Phenotypic Profiles." *Neuropsychology Review* 20, no. 1, pp. 103–120. doi:10.1007/s11065-009-9126-x

Wang, L.J., C.B. Yeh, Y.S. Huang, C.S. Tang, W.J. Chou, M.C. Chou, and C.K. Chen. 2012. "Neurocognitive Effects of Aripiprazole in Adolescents and Young Adults with Bipolar Disorder." *Nordic Journal of Psychiatry* 66, no. 4, pp. 276–82. doi:10.3109/08039488.2011.643484

Waugh, M.J., T.D. Meyer, E.A. Youngstrom, and J. Scott. 2014. "A Review of Self-Rating Instruments to Identify Young People at Risk for Bipolar Spectrum Disorders." *Journal of Affective Disorders* 160, pp. 113–121. doi:10.1016/j.jad.2013.12.019

Wechsler, D. 2009. *Wechsler Individual Achievement Test, Third edition (WIAT-III)*. San Antonio, TX: The Psychological Corporation.

Wechsler, D. 2011. *Wechsler Abbreviated Scale of Intelligence-Second Edition (WASI-II)*. San Antonio, TX: The Psychological Corporation.

Wechsler, D. 2013. *Wechsler Intelligence Scale for Children-Fourth Edition (WISC-IV)*. Bloomington, MN: Pearson.

Wechsler, D. 2014. *Wechsler Intelligence Scale for Children-Fifth Edition (WISC-V)*. Bloomington, MN: Pearson.

Wegbreit, E., G.K. Cushman, A.B. Weissman, E. Bojanek, K. Kim, E. Leibenluft, and D.Dickstein. 2016. "Reversal-Learning Deficits in Childhood-Onset Disorder Across the Transition from Childhood to Young Adulthood." *Journal of Affective Disorder* 203, pp. 46–54. doi:10.1016/j.jad.2016.05.046

Wegbreit, E., A.B. Weissman, G.K. Cushman, M.E. Puzia, K.L. Kim, E. Leibenluft, and D.P. Dickstein. 2015. "Facial Emotion Recognition in Childhood-Onset Bipolar I Disorder: An Evaluation of Developmental Differences Between Youths and Adults." *Bipolar Disorders* 17, pp. 471–85. doi:10.1111/bdi.12312

Weinstein, S.M., A. Van Meter, A.C. Katz, A.T. Peters, and A.W. West. 2015. "Cognitive and Family Correlates of Current Suicidal Ideation in Children with Bipolar Disorder." *Journal of Affective Disorders* 173. no. 1, pp. 15–21. doi:10.1016/j.jad.2014.10.058

Weissman, M.M., P. Wickramaratne, P. Adams, S. Wolk, H. Verdeli, and M. Olfson. 2000. "Brief Screening for Family Psychiatric History. The Family History Screen." *Archives of General Psychiatry* 57, no. 7, pp. 675–82.

West, A.E., R.H. Jacobs, R. Westerholm, A. Lee, J. Carbray, J. Heidenrich, and M.N. Pavuluri. 2009. "Child and Family-Focused Cognitive Behavioral Therapy for Pediatric Bipolar Disorder: Pilot Study of Group Treatment Format." *Journal of the Canadian Academy of Child and Adolescent Psychiatry* 18, no. 3, pp. 239–56.

West, A.E., and S.M. Weinstein. 2012. "A Family-Based Psychosocial Treatment Model." *Israel Journal of Psychiatry Related Science* 49, no. 2, pp. 86–93.

West, A.E., S.M. Weinstein, A.T. Peters, A.C. Katz, D.B. Henry, R.A Cruz, and M.N. Pavuluri. 2014. "Child- and Family-Focused Cognitive Behavioral Therapy for Pediatric Bipolar Disorder: A Randomized Clinical Trial." *Journal of the American Academy of Child & Adolescent Psychiatry* 53, no. 11, pp. 1168–78. doi:10.1016/j.jaac.2014.08.013

Whitney, J., J. Joormann, I.H. Gotlib, R.G. Kelley, T. Acquaye, M. Howe, and M.K. Singh. 2012. "Information Processing in Adolescents with Bipolar I Disorder." *Journal of Child Psychology & Psychiatry* 53, no. 9, pp. 937–45. doi:10.1111/j.1469-7610.2012.02543.x

Wilkinson, G.S., and G.J. Robertson. 2006. *Wide Range Achievement Test of Achievement: Fourth Edition (WRAT-4).* Lutz, FL: Psychological Assessment Resources, Inc. (PAR).

Woodcock, R., N. Mather, and K. McGrew. 2001. *Woodcock-Johnson III Tests of Achievement (WJ III ACH).* Rolling Meadows, IL: Riverside Publishing.

WHO (World Health Organization). 2016. Retrieved June 17, 2016 from http://www.who.int/en/

Wozniak, J., J. Biederman, M.K. Martelon, M.K. Hernandez, K.Y. Woodworth, and S.V. Faraone. 2013. "Does Sex Moderate the Clinical Correlates of Pediatric Bipolar-I Disorder? Results from a Large Controlled Family-Genetic Study." *Journal of Affective Disorders* 149, nos. 1–3. doi:10.1016/j.jad.2013.01.040

Wozniak, J., C.R. Petty, M. Schreck, A. Moses, S.V. Faraone, and J. Biederman. 2011. "High Level of Persistence of Pediatric Bipolar I Disorder from Childhood onto Adolescent Years: A Four Year Prospective Longitudinal Follow-Up Study." *Journal of Psychiatric Research* 45, no. 10, pp. 1273–82. doi:10.1016/j.jpsychires.2010.10.006

Yen, S., E. Frazier, H. Hower, L.M. Weinstock, D.R. Topor, J. Hunt, M.B. Keller. 2015. "Borderline Personality Disorder in Transition Age Youth with Bipolar Disorder." *Acta Psychiatrica Scandinavica* 132, no. 4, pp. 270–80. doi:10.1111/acps.12415

Yen, S., R. Stout, H. Hower, M.A. Killam, L.M. Weinstock, D.R. Topor, M.B. Keller. 2016. "The Influence of Comorbid Disorders on the Episodicity of Bipolar Disorder in Youth." *Acta Psychiatrica Scandinavica* 133, no. 4, pp. 324–34. doi:10.1111/acps.12514

Young, R., J. Biggs, V. Ziegler, and D. Myer. 1978. "A Rating Scale for Mania: Reliability, Validity and Sensitivity." *The British Journal of Psychiatry* 133, no. 5, pp. 429–35. doi:10.1192/bjp.133.5.429

Youngstrom, E.A. 2007. Pediatric Bipolar Disorder. In *Assessment of childhood disorders*, eds. E. Mash, and R. Barkley, 4th ed. New York: Guilford Press.

Youngstrom, E.A., and G.P. Algorta. 2014. Pediatric Bipolar Disorder. In *Child Psychopathology*, eds. E. Mash and R.A. Barkley, 3rd ed. New York: Guilford Press.

Youngstrom, E.A., B. Birmaher, and R.L. Findling. 2008. "Pediatric Bipolar Disorder: Validity, Phenomenology, and Recommendations for Diagnosis." *Bipolar Disorders* 10, no. 1 Pt 2, pp. 194–214. doi:10.1111/j.1399-5618.2007.00563.x

Youngstrom, E.A., R.L. Findling, C.K. Danielson, and J.R. Calabrese. 2001. "Discriminative Validity of Parent Report of Hypomanic and Depressive Symptoms on the General Behavior Inventory." *Psychological Assessment* 13, no. 2, pp. 267–76. doi:10.1037/1040-3590.13.2.267

Youngstrom, E.A., T.W. Frazier, C. Demeter, J.R. Calabrese, and R.L. Findling. 2008. "Developing a Ten Item Short Form of the Parent General Behavior Inventory to Assess for Juvenile Mania and Hypomania." *Journal of Clinical Psychiatry* 69, no. 5, pp. 831–39. doi:10.4088/JCP.v69n0517

Youngstrom, E.A., A.J. Freeman, and M.M. Jenkins. 2009. "The Assessment of Bipolar Disorder in Children and Adolescents." *Child and Adolescent Psychiatric Clinics of North America* 18, no. 2, pp. 359–90. doi:10.1016/j.chc.2008.12.002

Youngstrom, E.A., J.E. Genzlinger, G.A. Eagerton, and R.A. Van Meter. 2015. "Multivariate Meta-Analysis of the Discriminative Validity of Caregiver, Youth, and Teacher Rating Scales for Pediatric Bipolar Disorder: Mother Knows Best About Mania." *Archives of Scientific Psychology* 3, no. 1, pp. 112–37. doi:10.1037/arc0000024

Youngstrom, E.A., M.M. Jenkins, A. Jensen-Doss, and J.K. Youngstrom. 2012. "Evidence Based Assessment Strategies for Pediatric Bipolar Disorder." *Israel Journal of Psychiatry* 49, no. 1, pp. 15–27.

Youngstrom, E.A., O. Meyers, C.A. Demeter, J. Youngstrom, L. Morello, R. Piiparinen, R.L. Findling. 2005. "Comparing Diagnostic Checklists for Pediatric Bipolar Disorder in Academic and Community Mental Health Settings." *Bipolar Disorders* 7, no. 6, pp. 507–17. doi:10.1111/j.1399-5618.2005.00269.x

Youngstrom, E.A., O. Meyers, J.K. Youngstrom, J.R. Calabrese, and R.L. Findling. 2006. "Diagnostic and Measurement Issues in the Assessment of Pediatric Bipolar Disorder: Implications for Understanding Mood Disorders Across the Life Cycle." *Development and Psychopathology* 18, no. 4, pp. 989–1023. doi:10.1017/S0954579406060494

Youngstrom, E.A., G. Murray, S. Johnson, and R. Findling. 2013. "The 7 Up 7 Down Inventory: A 14-Item Measure of Manic and Depressive Tendencies Carved from the General Behavior Inventory." *Psychological Assessment* 25, no. 4, pp. 1377–83. doi:10.1037/a0033975

Youngstrom, E.A., J.K. Youngstrom, A.J. Freeman, A. De Los Reyes, N.C. Feeny, and R.L. Findling. 2011. "Informants Are Not all Equal: Predictors and Correlates of Clinical Judgments About Caregiver and Youth Credibility." *Journal of Child and Adolescent Psychopharmacology* 21, no. 5, pp. 407–15. doi:10.1089/cap.2011.0032

Youngstrom, E., J.K. Youngstrom, and M. Starr. 2005. "Bipolar Diagnoses in Community Mental Health: Achenbach Child Behavior Checklist Profiles and Patterns of Comorbidity." *Biological Psychiatry* 58, no. 7, pp. 569–75. doi:10.1016/j.biopsych.2005.04.004

Index

OTHER TITLES IN THIS CHILD CLINICAL PSYCHOLOGY "NUTS AND BOLTS" COLLECTION

Samuel T. Gontkovsky, *Editor*

Childhood and Adolescent Obesity
by Lauren Stutts

Intellectual Disabilities
by Charles J. Golden, Lisa K. Lashley, Andrew Grego,
Johanna Messerly, Ronald Okolichany, and Rachel Zachar

Learning Disabilities
by Charles J. Golden, Lisa K. Lashley, Jared S. Link,
Matthew Zusman, Maya Pinjala, Christopher Tirado, and Amber Deckard

Elimination Disorders: Evidence-Based Treatment for Enuresis and Encopresis
by Thomas M. Reimers

Depression in Childhood and Adolescence: A Guide for Practitioners
by Rebecca A. Schwartz-Mette, Hannah R. Lawrence,
Douglas W. Nangle, Cynthia A. Erdley, Laura Andrews,
and Melissa Jankowski